THE WALL STREET JOURNAL.

COMPLETE IDENTITY THEFT GUIDEBOOK

THE WALL STREET JOURNAL.

COMPLETE IDENTITY THEFT GUIDEBOOK

How to Protect Yourself from the Most
Pervasive Crime in America

TERRI CULLEN

THREE RIVERS PRESS
NEW YORK

Library of Congress Cataloging-in-Publication Data

Cullen, Terri.
   The Wall Street Journal complete identity theft guidebook : how to protect yourself from the most pervasive crime in America / Terri Cullen.
   1. Identity theft—United States—Prevention.   2. Consumer protection—United States.   I. Title.   II. Title: How to protect yourself from the most pervasive crime in America.
   HV6679.C85 2007
   362.88—dc22   2006034884

ISBN 978-0-307-33853-2

This book is dedicated to
my two greatest loves,
my husband, Gerry, and
our son, Gerald.

CONTENTS

INTRODUCTION
IT COULD
HAPPEN TO YOU

It could happen when you pull out your credit card at the mall, write a check at the grocery store or place an order online. In 2005 alone, about 8.9 million American adults discovered their personal information had been stolen and used to commit fraud. I was one of them. Fortunately, I was among the lucky ones and there was no financial toll, but it was an extremely upsetting event.

While the number of identity theft cases has been slowly declining over the years—down from 10.1 million in 2003—the size of losses is growing. The average theft resulted in a loss of $6,383 in 2005, up from $5,885 a year earlier, for a total loss of nearly $56.6 billion. The term "identity theft" covers several different specific crimes, and collectively, it is one of the easiest crimes to commit, one of the hardest to prosecute and one that is drawing increasing attention from the media.

No wonder you're reading this book! Like millions of other people, you're worried that it could happen to you and you don't know how to prevent it or what to do if you become a victim. Maybe the first time you'll be aware that someone is using your personal information illegally will be an unexplained charge on your monthly credit-card statement or a call from your credit-card issuer asking you if you've recently made several large purchases in a city you've never visited. In some cases, you may never know that your identity has been stolen and is being used by an illegal immigrant a thousand miles away so he or she can get work under a fraudulent Social Security number. In a nightmare scenario, you may find out the hard way, as did Abigail Kelly, a San Diego resident, who has sued her sister Delia—twice—for $50,000 after she discovered Delia had used her Social Security number to open fraudulent credit and utility accounts in her name. We'll learn more about Abigail's plight later in this book.

We tend to think of identity crimes as being committed by opportunists who steal our wallet or purse and use our credit cards to go on brief—but expensive—shopping sprees. There's plenty of that going on out there. But it may surprise you to know that almost half of those opportunistic crimes are committed by people we know, often relatives like Abigail Kelly's sister. Someone with a history of being fired from previous jobs for problems like theft or sexual harassment may "borrow" his more responsible big brother's or sister's name, Social Security number and other credentials to get another job.

While such one-on-one crimes are the most common, it's the dedicated criminal, intent on stealing personal information for use in committing a crime, who attracts the media attention when a case breaks. It might be an individual or a group of technology hackers who break into computers to steal information stored on the machine or install software programs that monitor your keyboard strokes for account and password information—all without your knowledge. Or the thief may be part of a group of criminals who simply buy the information from any number of unregulated legal or illegal sellers of sensitive consumer data, known as data brokers. Legitimate companies use the information to market products or run background checks on prospective customers or employees. Criminals can use the trove of information to commit virtually any type of identity theft or fraud.

At its core, identity theft is a violation of personal privacy that causes immense psychological distress. Victims haven't just lost cash or belongings, they've lost control of their own financial lives. Many aren't aware they've been robbed until it's too late, and the thief has already wreaked havoc on their personal and financial lives. Reclaiming control can be difficult, since stolen information can be used fraudulently again and again, sometimes by multiple criminals. Particularly draining are those cases involving perpetrators we know: parents or children, extended family members, neighbors, in-home employees or coworkers. Often, when a crime has been committed by a relative, a victim will find it emotionally difficult to report the crime or will be pressured by the family to keep the theft quiet. Even when thefts are small or when losses are covered by financial institutions, victims spend many frustrating hours notifying creditors, contacting credit-reporting agencies and, in some extreme cases, proving to skeptical law-enforcement officials that they've been victims of identity theft.

Unnerving, isn't it?

Well, the news isn't all bad. A survey done in 2006 found that nearly 70 percent of victims incurred no out-of-pocket expenses thanks to zero-liability offers extended by banks, credit unions and credit-card issuers. While the overall loss from each such incident averaged $6,383, the average out-of-pocket loss was just $422 because the financial institutions absorbed the rest. There's plenty most of us could do with $422, but a loss of that magnitude probably won't result in bankruptcy.

The media, of course, makes much of the huge amounts of data carelessly lost by companies and agencies or stolen from them. The U.S. Department of Veterans Affairs has had a particularly embarrassing run of bad luck. In May 2006, it lost one laptop computer that contained approximately 26.5 million names and other personal data. It recovered that one—only to lose another laptop a few months later. Fortunately, the risk of loss for victims of those security breaches is statistically low. It's simple math. It would take a thief an estimated forty years to exploit a million stolen IDs.

More importantly, individuals, companies and lawmakers

are becoming increasingly aware of the various ways in which identity theft can occur and are trying to take steps to prevent it and prosecute those who engage in it. Lawmakers have stepped up efforts to help protect individuals and assist victims. Identity theft officially became a federal crime in 1998, with the passage of the Identity Theft Assumption and Deterrence Act. Many states have also introduced stricter laws, with the state of California leading the nation in consumer-protection laws that not only help to prevent identity theft, but aid victims in recovery.

But don't relax yet. Identity theft poses a daunting problem. Passing laws doesn't help much for two reasons. First, many law enforcement agencies and prosecutors aren't interested in enforcing the laws at the local level because they would rather pursue crimes and criminals with a higher likelihood of conviction. More troublesome, perhaps, is that identity theft—particularly on the Internet—is extraordinarily difficult to trace, so perpetrators are seldom identified. Even when they are, there's a jurisdictional problem since the victim is usually in one place and the thief is somewhere else—sometimes in a foreign country.

Many experts believe the real solution to identity theft is going to be technological, not legal. And there's reason for some optimism in that arena, too. Techniques for enhancing data transactions over the Internet are being studied. Companies often have a vested interest in making their systems more secure, since they lose far more than their customers in most cases of identity fraud. Banks, for example, usually wind up defraying any customer losses due to identity theft. As a result, they're investing more money to adopt sophisticated antifraud technologies, and the efforts are paying off. Visa USA Inc. reported that risk-management techniques have cut fraud levels in half to six cents for every $100 processed, down from twelve cents a decade ago.

But many companies are more interested in protecting themselves than they are in protecting you. The banking and credit-card industries, for example, have actively lobbied against legislation that would restrict the use of your personal information to issue offers for new cards. Such legislation would have made it easier for you to prevent credit-card fraud. While they often will let you off the hook for debts incurred by someone fraudulently using your credit card, don't think it's out of kindness. Businesses are just accepting the losses as a cost of doing business, in their own interest of preventing more stringent restrictions on their operations.

This book is aimed first and foremost at helping you avoid becoming a victim. In the first section, I'll examine the myriad ways in which criminals steal identities, and the strategies and tactics you can use to keep them at bay. Some are obvious, but it's surprising how many people don't follow them. Others aren't so well known. For example, did you know the single most important tool you have to protect yourself from identity theft is your credit report? I'll dissect this critical document to show you what to look for and what to do if you find something amiss. Finally, for those of you who aren't tech geeks, I'll take an in-depth look at Internet scams and explain what steps you can take to foil criminals.

The second part of the book is devoted to the more common, and sometimes confusingly complex, situations that confront you when you find you've become a victim of identity theft. No question about it, you'll be frightened when you discover that unexplained $4,000 charge on your credit-card statement. But don't panic. There are many ways to go about fixing the problem and preventing recurrences.

After being burned, I now pay close attention to my credit-card statement online for signs of fraudulent charges, and when shopping online I always use a credit card, rather than my checking account's debit card. If things get more serious and you start getting calls from collection agents trying to dun you for debts you didn't incur, you can invoke an array of legal rights—probably more than you realize—to stop the harassment and fix the mistake. If worse comes to worst and you're arrested or charged with a crime committed by the person who stole your identity, there's advice on how to secure the proper legal counsel and what steps to take to clear your name.

Identity theft and identity fraud are huge problems, but they aren't the end of the world. Use the first part of this book to protect yourself, and you may never need to use the second half.

PART I

PREVENTING IDENTITY THEFT

CHAPTER 1

WHAT IS IDENTITY THEFT, ANYWAY?

Jerome Powell remembers being irritated with himself for not paying closer attention to his driving. When the Mountain View, Colorado, police car's lights came on behind him, Powell, a government contractor, had just driven through a yellow light as it turned red. Now he would be late for his next appointment. He apologized to the officer and handed over his driver's license and insurance information. He watched in his rearview mirror as the officer radioed from his cruiser for a license check.

It seemed to be taking a long time to write a routine ticket. Finally, the officer approached Powell's window and told him to get out of the car. Powell was stunned to find himself under arrest on an outstanding warrant. He was shocked and humiliated as the officer made him put his hands behind his back and then cuffed him and read him his Miranda rights. The Navy veteran spent hours in jail, shaking from fear that he might wind up charged with a crime he didn't commit.

The warrant for his arrest was issued in 2003, when a thief used Powell's driver's license to buy more than $10,000 in computer equipment and other items. Despite overwhelming evidence that it was a case of identity theft—the stolen goods were delivered to the apartment of a career criminal who bore no resemblance at all to Powell—he was forced to spend several thousand dollars to post bond and get a lawyer to clear his name.

Jerome Powell's unnerving and expensive experience is a true case of identity theft—the thief used Powell's driver's license to impersonate Powell. Not to be picky about it, but what the media and most people call "identity theft" is actually an umbrella term for two different crimes: identity theft and identity fraud. As in Powell's case, identity theft occurs when criminals steal personal information and use it to impersonate the victim. An illegal immigrant using a stolen Social Security card to get a job is a good example of such an impersonation, as is a driver who has lost his or her license because of multiple convictions for driving while intoxicated and buys a fake driver's license from an underground dealer containing the name and information of an identity-theft victim. True identity theft accounts for about a third of the 685,000 identity crime complaints reported to the Federal Trade Commission in 2005.

Far more common is identity fraud. It happens when thieves obtain a victim's sensitive personal information to steal money from bank accounts, buy goods and services with existing credit-card accounts or use the data to open new credit lines. The shocking thing is that these types of criminals are frequently people we know. Such betrayals by family or close friends are emotionally draining and almost certainly underreported, since victims often find it difficult to report the crime or feel pressured by family members to keep the theft quiet.

Not Abigail Kelly. Abigail had given her Social Security number to her sister Delia after Delia said she was going to make Abigail the beneficiary of her life-insurance policy. Delia promptly used Abigail's information to open fraudulent credit and utility accounts. As a result, Abigail not only suffered damage to her credit history, but she didn't get the job after an em-

IDENTITY THEFT IS NOTHING NEW

Identity theft is a crime most people associate with the Internet age, but imposters have been assuming the identities of others throughout time. Identity theft has often been used as a means to gain power. Pretenders to the European and Russian thrones once were very common. In the mid-14th century, as many as four people attempted to take on the persona of Portugal's King Sebastian, both in his country and abroad. In the 15th century, at least two imposters came very close to taking the throne of Russian tsar Dmitriy Ivanovich. The Roman Catholic Church uses the term "antipope" to describe people who make widely supported claims that they are the Pope.

Impersonating other people for financial gain began long before the introduction of credit cards and the Internet. In one of the most outrageous examples of identity theft in the early 20th century, conman Victor Lustig adopted the persona of a top French official using forged government documents. He then "sold" the Eiffel Tower to an unsuspecting scrap-metal dealer in 1925. The tower was badly in need of repair and Lustig managed to convince the dealer that the government had decided to do away with the landmark and sell it for scrap. (He even got the dealer to pay him a bribe to sell it!) Most recently, filmmaker Steven Speilberg made a movie based on the life of Frank Abagnale Jr., a teenage con artist who in the mid-1960s stole almost $40,000 by printing his own bank-account number on blank bank deposit slips, which were processed right along with legitimate deposit slips. His life was portrayed in the 2002 motion picture *Catch Me If You Can*.

ployee background check turned up an arrest warrant in her name in Maine. Abigail had never even been to Maine. But Delia lived there. Abigail later learned that her sister was behind numerous accounts opened in her name, though Delia wasn't arrested or charged with any crime. Local law enforcement refused to get involved in what looked like a family dispute, so Abigail wound up suing her sister in civil court instead. After Abigail sued her—once in California and again in Maine—Delia finally agreed to pay most of the $50,000, but the incident tore their relationship apart. "You are dead to me," Delia later told Abigail.

Routine one-on-one crimes are the most common and are largely ignored by the media and, unfortunately, many times by law enforcement. It's the big-time scams and plots that get the attention. In August 2005, employees at Sunbelt Software Inc. stumbled upon a massive identity-theft ring while researching "CoolWebSearch," a dangerous software program that hijacks Internet servers and Web home pages—as well as other browser applications. The software was routinely obtaining and broadcasting data such as individual names, bank-account numbers, passwords and PINs, and other extremely sensitive personal information from millions of infected computers. That investigation continues today.

It's surprisingly easy to become an identity thief or fraudster by joining the ranks of criminals who simply buy the information from any number of legal or illegal sellers of sensitive consumer data. Once little-known to most Americans, the data-broking industry burst into the spotlight in February 2005, when ChoicePoint, a seller of consumer data to financial institutions and government agencies, disclosed that criminals posing as legitimate businesspeople had purchased personal information on 145,000 people. (Later, the figure was revised to 162,000.) Americans were staggered by the types of personal information being sold by ChoicePoint, including their names, their spouses' names, current and previous addresses, phone numbers, Social Security numbers, names of employers and even information about family members and neighbors. While individuals can sometimes buy such data legally, most legitimate data brokers sell only to corporate customers. But the fact that there's little regulation of legal data sales means it's easier for criminals to get their hands on your information.

COMPANIES RESPOND TO DATA BREACHES

Here's a sampling of what some specific companies and organizations have offered to do in response to disclosures that sensitive consumer information was lost or stolen from their databases.

Time Warner

A contractor moving backup tapes discovered that computer tapes containing data, including many Social Security numbers, on 600,000 current and former employees, were missing. Time Warner offered a year of free credit-monitoring service.

Fidelity Investments

A Fidelity employee's laptop, containing personal information on 196,000 current and former Hewlett-Packard workers, was stolen from a rental car. In response, the fund giant alerted credit-reporting agencies and offered free credit-monitoring service for a year to current and former HP employees.

Tufts University

Administrators discovered unusual activity on a university-owned computer with data, including some Social Security numbers, on 106,000 alumni. Tufts set up an 800 number for assistance and encouraged people to put alerts on their credit reports, but did not offer to pay for monitoring.

University of California, Berkeley

A stolen laptop containing Social Security numbers belonging to as many as 98,000 students, alumni and applicants. UC Berkeley set up a hotline and encouraged people to put alerts on their credit reports, but didn't offer to pay for monitoring.

Wells Fargo

Four computers containing sensitive personal data for thousands of people were stolen from a vendor that prints loan statements. Wells Fargo responded by offering a year of free credit monitoring using its own service.

Source: The Wall Street Journal. Online

Over the last five years, media coverage has increased as dozens of companies, universities, government agencies and other organizations have reported that vast amounts of sensitive consumer information was either lost or stolen. The list of companies that have reported lost or stolen consumer information reads like a "Who's Who" of big business: Bank of America, Fidelity, Time Warner, Verizon and Wells Fargo, among others. In some instances, data-storage tapes went missing or laptops containing sensitive information were stolen; in others, employees of the companies or organizations obtained unauthorized access to the information. Even the federal government isn't immune. In 2006, thieves stole data on about 26.5 million military personnel from the U.S. Department of Veterans Affairs. The laptop with the missing data was recovered, and two teens were arrested for the theft. But the department stumbled twice more, first when it canceled the credit-monitoring service it had offered the victims of the laptop theft, infuriating innumerable veterans who were counting on it to help protect the breach of their sensitive information. And then it happened again! Another department laptop, containing information on up to 38,000 veterans, disappeared. Needless to say, there are some decidedly unhappy vets wondering just how inept the department can get.

Not surprisingly, victims are beginning to fight back in the courts against companies and organizations that report breaches of sensitive consumer data. In June 2006, a coalition of veterans' groups filed a suit against the federal government in the U.S. District Court in Washington, D.C., seeking $1,000 in damages for each of the roughly 26.5 million military personnel, both current and former, whose data was on the stolen laptop mentioned earlier. The case is ongoing. In July 2005, a group of plaintiffs filed a class-action lawsuit in California Superior Court against CardSystems Solutions Inc. after the company disclosed that computer hackers had obtained data on about 250,000 credit- and debit-card accounts. This case is also ongoing.

GARDEN VARIETY IDENTITY FRAUD

I'll get into some of the more exotic types of identity theft and fraud later. For the moment, let's take a look at some of the most common forms of identity crimes. It isn't hard to guess that by far the favored tool of identity thieves is the ubiquitous credit card. We all have them and we love to use them. So do identity thieves. The Federal Trade Commission (FTC) found that 26 percent of all complaints of identity fraud in 2005 involved fraudulent charges on an existing account or new accounts opened using lost or stolen consumer information.

How easy is it to fall victim to credit-card fraud? Let me count the ways.

We use credit cards so often and in so many places— online and in person—that it is almost impossible to avoid tripping up and revealing your account information to a potential thief. I shudder to think of how careless I was with my credit-card account information before I discovered that I'd become the victim of identity fraud. I would routinely crumple up credit-card receipts containing my signature and entire account number and then casually toss them in the nearest trash receptacle for a would-be thief to snatch. When making travel reservations at work, I'd broadcast my credit-card number when giving it out to hotels or car-rental agencies, and so anyone within the sound of my voice could jot it down. When using ATMs, I worried more about the guy behind me invading my personal space than I did about whether the offending person was "shoulder surfing" to learn my account's password. Online, I remembered— occasionally—to check to see if a site's Web address started

> ## TOP FIVE MOST COMMON TYPES OF FRAUD
>
> - Credit-card fraud
> - Phone or utilities fraud
> - Bank fraud
> - Employment fraud
> - Government documents/ benefits fraud
>
> Source: Federal Trade Commission

with the telltale "https://" and the tiny closed-padlock symbol at the bottom of the Web browser that indicated I was shopping at a secure site. I almost never checked sites such as the Better Business Bureau (www.bbbonline.org) and TRUSTe (www.truste.com) to ensure that the Web site I was using was a legitimate business.

Then a phone call from my credit-card issuer made me aware of just how easy it is to fall victim to identity fraud. The company's representative said the company noticed I'd made two purchases within hours of each other using my card—one in New York, the other in France. Fortunately for me, the card company put the purchases on hold until it could contact me and verify that I had made them. I was shocked—and a little scared. If my credit-card information had been stolen, what other personal information could the thief have?

So now I pay close attention to things like keeping my voice down when making travel reservations or making sure no one gets too close in the ATM line. I also routinely monitor my credit-card statements online for signs of fraudulent charges. When shopping online, I always use a credit card, rather than my debit card, which is attached to my checking account, because federal law limits liability for unauthorized credit-card use to $50 per card—though many companies will waive this amount if they are notified of the charge in a timely manner. Some debit cards don't have this kind of zero-liability protection against fraud, but, more importantly, even if your bank offers zero-liability coverage on your checking account, it could take weeks to recover your account after a thief has wiped it out—and you could find yourself vulnerable to bounced-check fees on outstanding payments.

CALLING ALL THIEVES

After credit-card fraud, phone, cable and utilities fraud is the second most common form of identity theft, making up 18 percent of all complaints reported. Dishonest people steal per-

HIJACKING YOUR INTERNET PHONE SERVICE

 Internet calling has been a boon for consumers yearning for inexpensive online phone service, but weaknesses in its security have been a boon for hackers and thieves. Federal authorities arrested the head of two small Miami telecom companies and a Spokane, Washington, computer programmer in 2006 for hacking into the networks of as many as fifteen other Internet phone providers to fraudulently route customers' calls, according to a federal complaint filed in New Jersey. The case is ongoing.

According to the suit, the defendants had sold deeply discounted packages of Internet phone minutes and scanned the networks of unsuspecting companies, searching for weak spots through which to route those calls. The companies carried the calls while the defendants collected more than $1 million in connection fees, according to the suit. The defendants were allegedly able to obtain the "prefixes," or proprietary codes, that are established by telecom companies to accept calls for routing. Using a method called "brute force," they flooded the telecom providers with test calls, each carrying a different prefix, until they found a match. The defendants also hacked into companies' computers so they could route their customers' calls through them and disguise the calls' origin. One Newark, New Jersey, Internet phone company was billed for more than 500,000 unauthorized calls.

Source: The Wall Street Journal.

sonal information in order to apply for cell-phone contracts or improperly gain access to cable, telephone, gas and electric energy, or other types of utilities. It's a difficult crime to combat, which is why it's so popular among identity thieves. They open accounts in one place and then quickly move on to the next to avoid capture. By the time victims discover the crimes, the thief is usually long gone.

Kevin Scott of Philadelphia discovered he was the victim of utility fraud when he requested a copy of his credit report after being denied credit. A thief had obtained Scott's Social Security number and used it to open utility accounts at several addresses, racking up thousands of dollars in phone, cable, gas and electric bills. The utility companies allowed the criminal to open these accounts despite the fact that duplicate accounts already existed in Scott's name at his true address. They also never bothered to contact him. He spent hundreds of hours clearing his good name. He was also frustrated because state and local law enforcers refused to help him track down the thief, despite the fact that authorities had his picture on file after the thief obtained a Pennsylvania driver's license using Scott's name.

TAKE IT TO THE BANK

Bank fraud is only slightly less common than utilities fraud, which is surprising given that banks are among the more security-conscious businesses—and fooling around with a bank can earn a thief a visit from the Federal Bureau of Investigation. Bank fraud accounts for 17 percent of reported identity-theft cases, with nearly 2 million Americans reporting that thieves transferred funds out of their checking accounts in 2004. The average loss per incident was $1,200. Fortunately, consumers rarely are left holding the bag. If the fraud is reported promptly, most banks won't hold the customer liable for losses resulting from the crime. While fraudulent loans accounted for some bank fraud, the most frequent types of fraud involved electronic funds transfers and forged checks.

Mailboxes are the venue of choice for bank fraudsters. It isn't difficult to recognize a box of checks sitting in a mailbox, although it takes a diligent thief to check dozens of mailboxes on any given day to find the occasional box of checks. More sophisticated thieves look for bill-payment envelopes left in the mailbox for pickup—then use special chemicals to erase the ink and insert different names.

But the electronic age has taken bank fraud high-tech. The explosion of electronic-payment services over the last ten years has led to a rash of account hijackings, which occur when a thief steals a bank account owner's user name and password and then accesses the accounts online in order to make illegal electronic funds transfers. With more entities gaining direct access to bank-account owners' account numbers and pass-words, there's a growing opportunity for in-house employees or hackers to steal bank information and hijack accounts.

More recently, law-enforcement officials have begun cracking down on ATM fraud. Thieves insert tiny cameras into ATM kiosks—typically the kind you'd find at gas stations or convenience stores—to steal account numbers and PINs. The suspects then transfer the account data to separate cards with magnetic strips and use the new cards and PINs to empty the victims' accounts. One ATM ring busted in the San Francisco Bay area in 2006 highlighted the potential damage this type of fraud can inflict: Just one kiosk in a network of seven obtained account information on at least ninety people, who eventually had more than $110,000 stolen from their accounts.

PRETENDERS TO YOUR NAME

The next major category of theft involves thieves who steal sensitive information from people looking for work and then pretend to be someone else by using the illegally obtained Social Security numbers and other identifying information in order to find a job. Among the tricks scammers use to get job seekers to give out sensitive personal information is to pose as prospective employers. The phony ads can often be very convincing, with thieves copying the wording on postings by well-respected corporate Web sites to make "job candidates" feel more comfortable about sharing their information. Other con artists pose as job-recruiters, offering for a fee to provide

PROTECT YOURSELF AGAINST "PRETEXTING"

The boardroom intrigue at Hewlett-Packard, in which the computer giant admitted an investigator it hired used "pretexting" to obtain board members' personal phone records, has reignited concerns about the controversial practice.

Pretexters use personal information, such as a birth date and Social Security number, to impersonate someone and contact companies the victim does business with. Pretexters want information, such as phone call logs, credit-card purchases and brokerage statements, for use in such things as private investigations or legal and divorce proceedings. In other cases, pretexting can lead to identity theft, where a criminal uses the accessed information to steal from existing accounts or open new ones.

Even mundane information, such as what movies a person has rented, can be dangerous in the wrong hands. "Even if you think it's the most boring information in the world, there's someone out there who can exploit the information for profit," says Lillie Coney, associate director of the Electronic Privacy Information Center in Washington, D.C.

The best way to prevent someone from viewing account information without permission is to do business with companies with strong privacy protections in place. Where once all that was needed was a Social Security number or account number to access personal information by phone or online, many companies now require additional information.

"About a year ago we stopped using Social Security numbers because we felt they were just too readily available," says Eric Rabe, a spokesman for Verizon Communications Inc. Now Verizon customer-service reps require a specific account code on the customer's monthly paper bill before giving out account information or making changes to the account.

Companies such as Bank of America Corp. and Vanguard Group let customers choose passwords and images and answer challenge questions, which customers must provide if they attempt to log into their accounts from personal computers that the companies don't recognize as ones they've used before.

It's rare that companies will allow customers to block their account from being viewed online by anyone (even the account holder), so consumers must take an active role in protecting their information from pretexters.

If you receive monthly statements or bills in the mail, buy a cross-cut shredder and shred them before you put them in the trash. Even if you don't view account statements online, register for online access—before a pretexter uses your information to do it for you.

Creating passwords that are tough to crack can help. Chapter 3 offers tips on how to create hacker-resistant passwords. If you're asked to choose a "challenge question"—a question to which only you might know the answer and that would verify that you are who you say you are—choose the one that's the most obscure. For example, "What was the name of your favorite teacher?"

If the companies you do business with have lax privacy guards, demand better protection—or take your business elsewhere.

Source: The Wall Street Journal. Online

"services" they never render and then making off with their victims' identifying data.

The latest wrinkle in employment fraud involves thieves posing as background-check firms that trick job seekers into providing a wealth of sensitive personal information. A typical scheme starts with the thief obtaining names from job-search agencies or Web sites. Then a victim is asked to provide everything from his or her height, weight and eye color to Social Security number and mother's maiden name.

Not surprisingly, identity theft is being used as a tool for illegal immigrants to obtain employment in the United States using stolen Social Security numbers. The increasingly sophisticated forged documents make it tough for companies to verify whether they're legitimate, and the documents are easy to come by. Immigrant sympathizers and forgery rings that operate just across the border in Mexico generate thousands of

Sentry Security Co., Inc.
1130 Avenue of the Americas
New York, NY 10001

SCREENING APPLICATION

First name: _____

Middle name:_____

Last name: _____

Address: _____

Date of birth: _____

Age: _____ Height: _____ Weight: _____

Hair color: _____ Eye color: _____

Social Security number: _____-_____-_____

Mother's maiden name: _____

Unsuspecting job candidates are duped into filling out forms similar to the one above.

fake Social Security cards and green cards that look authentic. But the federal government is cracking down and has set up a verification system to help companies spot identity thieves. When large companies hire new workers, many electronically send the job candidate's name, Social Security number, address and citizenship status to the U.S. Department of Homeland Security, where its pilot system compares the information against government data and either confirms that the new hire is eligible to work in the United States or warns the company that there may be something wrong. For example, if the person's name doesn't match the name on file for a given Social Security number, a red flag goes up. Unfortunately, companies aren't required by law to run these types of checks, and many smaller firms in need of workers for hard-to-place labor jobs would rather give their employees the benefit of the doubt.

Fraudulent use of Social Security numbers is often hard to detect unless the user makes a glaring mistake. That happened to Elena Ma Santana Contreras when she applied for a position at an employment center in Butler County, Ohio. A routine check of her Social Security number revealed that it belonged to a male military veteran. Unable to explain the obvious gender discrepancy, she was arrested and her case is pending.

Unfortunately, the problem is often bigger than an individual looking for a job with a stolen Social Security number. In a case in 2005, members of a Mexican-based crime ring were indicted by U.S. officials on charges of fraud, conspiracy and identity theft. The group was charged with manufacturing fake IDs and immigration documents, including stolen driver's licenses and Social Security numbers. The individuals indicted were living in the United States and working with their counterparts in Mexico. The case is ongoing.

As these examples might lead you to suspect, protecting yourself from this kind of crime isn't easy. It's likely you'll never know that someone is using your Social Security number to obtain work unless the thief used the number to open financial accounts in your name or to commit other crimes. When someone uses your Social Security number to obtain a job, that employer would report the wages the thief earns in your name on a W-2. The phantom earnings would also appear on your annual Social Security statement. While this may appear to be a good thing—bigger earnings mean a larger Social Security check down the road—there can be some troubling consequences. You might receive a notice from the IRS alleging that you underreported your income and be held liable for any taxes due. If the thief files a tax return and receives a tax refund in your name, the IRS may deny your own tax return and refund.

You'd think the Social Security Administration or the IRS would have a verification system in place that would make it obvious the Social Security number is being used illegally, but unfortunately they don't. It's up to you to check your Social Security earnings record at www.ssa.gov/mystatement, or request a copy at (800) 772-1213. If your statement indicates that you are earning more than you do, contact the Social Security Administration to report potential fraud.

DOCUMENTS AND BENEFITS

Another major area of identity theft reported by the Federal Trade Commission (FTC) in 2005 involved government documents and benefits fraud (9 percent), where thieves fraudulently applied for and received Social Security and Medicare cards and benefits. In 2006, Charles Hood was convicted for using false Social Security numbers to collect more than $23,000 in workers' compensation benefits. Hood (also known as Charles Byrd) pleaded guilty to unemployment fraud and workers' compensation fraud and was sentenced to two-and-a-half years in prison. He was also forced to make full restitution. The investigation found that between 1980 and 1997 Hood had made workers' compensation claims using different Social Security numbers under the names Hood and Byrd. In February 2002, Hood began collecting unemployment benefits after being laid off from a construction company, and in October of that same year he continued to collect benefits after he found another job.

In 2003, Jorge Rio Mejia and nine other people were sentenced in a benefits-theft ring in Fresno County, California. According to the indictment, the thieves broke into the offices of payroll-service companies and raided their trash bins to steal their clients' employee information. The group then allegedly filed for benefits using the stolen data and routed the checks to post office boxes throughout the country. Before being caught, the group allegedly defrauded the government out of $2.8 million. The case is pending.

Unfortunately, it's unlikely you'll discover that someone is using your information to fraudulently collect benefits until you need to collect them yourself. Because there are limits on the amount of benefits you're entitled to receive, you could potentially find yourself with limited access to benefits that were rightfully yours.

LAX LAW ENFORCEMENT

You've probably noticed as you've been reading this chapter that the victims aren't getting a lot of sympathy or help from law-enforcement agencies. Why does such a widespread crime get such short shrift from police and prosecutors? A lot of it has to do with the nature of the crime. Many identity crimes are two-step crimes, meaning one person steals the information— such as a credit-card number or Social Security number—and sells it to another person, who then uses it to make fraudulent transactions. And even in cases in which the same person steals the information and uses it illegally, recall that many credit-card fraud cases involve victims who know the identity of the thieves are family members or close friends. There's a natural reluctance on the part of law enforcement to get caught in a family feud, as we saw in Abigail Kelly's case. Often the victim has second thoughts before a trial starts and drops the charge, making officers reluctant to spend their time, money and energy on these cases. What's more, most law-enforcement agencies don't have investigators experienced in identity theft or fraud, and some won't investigate frauds if only a small amount is lost or the victim can't prove to officials that a crime has been committed.

But a bigger reason identity thieves avoid prosecution is that modern forms of identity theft are extremely difficult to police. First, the criminal moves swiftly. Fraudulent Internet sites that lure people into disclosing personal data are kept open for an average of only five or six days, which gives law-enforcement officers a very short time frame to make a case. More importantly, the crime takes place through a computer server, which can be located anywhere in the world. That not only makes the detective work even more difficult, it also creates jurisdictional problems if and when the perpetrators are identified. What's illegal in the United States isn't necessarily illegal in other countries.

Federal agencies have stepped in to try to help local law-enforcement agencies share information on identity-theft crimes in an effort to crack down on these crimes and better assist victims. The Federal Trade Commission has created the Identity Theft Data Clearinghouse for tracking complaints. Once the agency receives a complaint from a victim, it analyzes the complaint and then clusters it with similar cases. That information is then made available to federal and local law enforcers to assist with investigations and criminal trials.

Many states are trying harder to help their own residents prevent identity theft and combat fraud. California was the first state to require banks and other companies that do business in the state to notify customers when their information is lost or stolen, and to require businesses to truncate and otherwise protect Social Security numbers from being viewed. The ChoicePoint incident—and the hundreds of companies that stepped forward afterward to disclose consumer information that was lost or stolen—probably would not have been reported if it weren't for the California laws. In the wake of the highly publicized data breaches, many other states criminalized identity theft and instituted their own data-breach notification laws. And a number of states, including California, New York, Pennsylvania and Texas, have set up their own task forces to focus on tracking and solving identity-theft crimes.

Still, identity thieves are so elusive that the chances of catching them are small. Because of this, the businesses most affected by identity theft—banks, credit-card companies and retailers—are increasingly using technology to monitor consumer accounts for potential signs of fraud and are then alerting consumers to suspicious activity in order to prevent losses. Such monitoring technology uses sophisticated algorithms to figure out when there are deviations from the normal ways in which a consumer uses his or her credit card. My credit-card issuer's computers probably didn't have a hard time figuring out that I wouldn't be using the card almost simultaneously in New York and in France. But when a friend recently bought some appliances from Sears, which makes consumers pay at separate counters for stoves and refrigerators, his issuer's computers questioned such rapid use of his card and halted the transactions. He was grateful the issuer was on guard, but irritated that it took an hour of back-and-forth phone calls to okay the purchase.

If you're really serious about protecting your identity, you can, in some states, put a freeze on your credit report. Many states, including Florida, New York, New Jersey, Illinois and California, have enacted laws that allow consumers to issue a "credit freeze" that blocks any prospective lender, including banks, mortgage companies, car dealers and credit-card issuers, from issuing new credit in a consumer's name without permission. It's a strong step toward giving you control of your identity. Dumpster divers who recover your data from garbage bags and try to open a credit-card account in your name will have a tough time doing it if you have a credit freeze on your credit report.

But not everyone is on your side in the battle against identity theft—even those who should be. The credit-reporting bureaus and financial institutions are in the business of selling credit-card information, and the banks and other issuers are in the business of marketing credit cards to consumers, so anything that prevents them from doing either hurts their business. Those industries have lobbied in support of a bill introduced by Rep. Steve LaTourette (R, Ohio) that would effectively revoke a consumer's rights to issue a credit freeze unless a person has been the victim of a crime (any crime resulting from the theft of personal information)! At the time of writing, the bill, titled The Financial Data Protection Act of 2006, was still under consideration, and several consumer groups were pointing out how it would undermine consumer protection. There's no question that if it passes, it will be a step backward in the fight against identity theft.

Now that we've gotten a broad overview of what identity theft is all about, let's look at the people involved, both the thieves and their victims.

CHAPTER 2

THINKING LIKE A THIEF

Who are these people who steal our identities and what makes them tick?

It's impossible to come up with a one-size-fits-all description of identity thieves because the nature of the crime itself is so diverse. A thief may be an uneducated immigrant desperate for a fake Social Security card and driver's license so he or she will have a better chance of finding work. Or he or she could be a drug addict trading stolen credit cards and driver's licenses for methamphetamines. Then there's the computer enthusiast who creates programs to hack into computer databases and steal sensitive information for profit. A sizable number of thieves are foreign gangsters running globe-girdling enterprises with armies of employees who use an array of methods to steal identities. Most disturbing is that the thief might be our brother, sister, father or mother who "borrow" our identity to get a job, buy a car or open a credit-card account.

No matter the motivations, they're drawn to identity theft because it's easy, it's lucrative and it's low-risk. The one thing we know for sure about the thieves is that the best of them are becoming increasingly bold and ingenious in executing their schemes.

Jonathan Turley, a law professor at George Washington University in Washington, D.C., says identity thieves are often hard to locate, and many times the crimes involve only small losses. "There is little glory or publicity in prosecuting identity-theft cases," he told *The Wall Street Journal*. Mr. Turley was a victim of identity theft himself after his Social Security number was stolen from files at CBS News, where he worked as a legal analyst. He says he was told by FBI agents and New York police detectives that thieves are rarely prosecuted because district attorneys want more high-profile cases.

A THIEF FOR EVERY OCCASION

The best way to understand the immense diversity of identity thieves is to look at the ways in which they work. Consider first what I call the "traditionalist" thief, who uses tried and true methods to obtain personal information, including the following:

- Stealing a briefcase, wallet or purse from your home or car.

- Lifting checks from a checkbook carelessly left out on a counter.

- Taking bank account or credit-card statements, new checks, pre-approved credit or loan offers, medical bills or retirement-account information from a mailbox or garbage can.

- Stealing information contained in your employment records from your employer's mailbox or garbage can—also known as "dumpster diving."

- Tricking you into giving him or her your information over the phone or in person by posing as a legitimate charity or company with whom you do business.

- Filling out a change of address form with the U.S. Postal Service to divert documents to a different address.

- "Shoulder surfing," or eavesdropping on people giving out their financial-account numbers, Social Security number or date of birth over the phone, or watching people as they enter password or account information at a bank or an ATM.

Then there are those I call the "early adopters" who work the Internet and the complex unseen world of electronic funds transfers to snoop for sensitive information in other ways:

- "Hacking"—A person breaks into computers to steal information stored on the machine or to install malicious software programs that monitor your keyboard strokes for account and password information.

- "Phishing"—One source says the word is derived from "password harvesting fishing." This is the use of e-mail and Web sites designed to look like those of legitimate companies, mainly banks, to trick consumers into divulging financial-account and password information.

- "Skimming"—This is a technique that uses a data-storage device to capture credit- or debit-card numbers after the card is swiped to make a legitimate purchase or bank-account withdrawal at an ATM.

- Posing as an employer, landlord, creditor or other individual who may have the legal right to access your credit report from one of the three major credit agencies: Experian, Equifax and TransUnion.

- Creating fake checks, credit cards or debit cards with stolen personal information using technology that can readily be purchased online for reproducing official-looking identification cards.

- Simply purchasing the information from any number of online data brokers and trafficking firms that sell the data, legally or illegally.

In some ways, it's amazing there aren't more cases of identity theft, considering how easy it is to become a victim. Any clerk, cashier or waiter deals with dozens of credit cards every day on the job and could easily jot down the card's number and set up shop as a small-time identity thief.

DON'T BE AN EASY VICTIM

But the real money lies not in the theft of one or two credit cards—the chances are high that the card's legitimate owner will notice the fraudulent billings and cancel the card—but in the gathering of masses of personal data that can then be re-marketed to illegal data-brokering networks. Fledgling identity thieves often get into the business by "dumpster diving," retrieving sacks of trash from dumpsters and sorting through it looking for tidbits of personal information, such as canceled checks, credit-card or bank statements or health-care statements that contain Social Security numbers.

Experian, one of the three big credit-reporting agencies, did its own dumpster diving to see how easy it is for criminals to acquire your sensitive consumer information. After digging through four hundred household garbage bins, the results were staggering: More than 70 percent of the bags contained the individual's full name and address. About 40 percent of the bags contained a whole credit-card or debit-card number that could be linked to a specific individual, and 80 percent of those numbers included the cards' expiration dates. About 20 percent of the bags held a bank-account number and sort code that could be linked to an individual's name and address, and one bag even contained a signed, blank check! Only 14 percent of the bags contained nothing of interest to a criminal. Dumpster diving isn't illegal. In fact, there are plenty of people who go diving to find and recycle knick-knacks and other things someone else is throwing away. (One person's trash really is another's treasure!) A crime occurs only when someone who has obtained personal information from a sack of trash then *uses* that information fraudulently.

Dumpster diving is small potatoes compared to a sophisticated "phishing" operation. Phishing schemes combine the brains of malicious computer code writers with the marketing skills of con artists to come up with sophisticated-looking phony e-mails that are sent out by the millions in an effort to get victims to reveal account information. A successful phishing expedition can bring in hundreds of detailed responses from unsuspecting victims who readily divulge passwords, PINs and, yes, their mother's maiden name.

Eventually the information garnered by thieves shows up for sale on Web sites, many run out of the former Soviet Union or Eastern Europe, where regulation and enforcement is scanty or nonexistent. The more detailed the personal information— credit-card data that includes "MMN," or mother's maiden name, is particularly prized—the higher the price thieves pay for the stolen data.

The purloined card data is purchased by a variety of entrepreneurial thieves, some of whom use the information to buy merchandise from legitimate sources, such as eBay, for re-marketing. Others use it for thrills or personal purchases. One New York teenager now serving time after being arrested three times for identity theft used stolen card data to buy expensive auto parts and to treat his girlfriend to luxurious weekends in New York's finest hotels, often in suites costing thousands of dollars. He told reporters that he knew it was wrong, but that because it was so easy to do, he couldn't avoid the temptation. Now he's worried that when he's released from prison, the temptation will again be too powerful to resist.

INNOVATIONS IN IDENTITY THEFT

Stolen credit-card data is a huge business and very difficult to stop, but it's been around for a long time. Now identity thieves are getting more clever and creative, as demonstrated by some of the newer methods they're employing to use our data for their own gain. Some of the scams sound nearly impossible to pull off—until you read about the growing numbers of victims who once felt the same way.

Bankruptcy fraud is an interesting twist on credit theft and can take many forms. Often, the people who commit this type of fraud are known to the victims—a parent, an adult child or other close relative or acquaintance. In one typical scam, the imposter will use a victim's name and Social Security number to open fraudulent credit accounts, run up debt and then file for bankruptcy to wipe out the debts.

That's what happened to twenty-four-year-old Randy Waldron Jr. He discovered he was the victim of bankruptcy fraud when he was turned down for his first credit card because of bad credit history. But Randy didn't have a credit history—or so he thought. Unknown to Randy, his father, whom he hadn't seen since he was a young child, had used Randy's name and Social Security number to run up tens of thousands of dollars of debt before filing for bankruptcy in Randy's name.

But his father didn't stop there—he was also convicted of three felonious assault and battery charges under his assumed identity. In total, Waldron Sr. ran up more than $2 million in debt and judgments in his son's name. Young Randy spent countless hours clearing his name.

In another scheme, the imposter is someone whose home is in jeopardy of foreclosure. The homeowner transfers the property into the name of the victim, who is usually someone the thief knows, and then files for bankruptcy in that person's name to avoid foreclosure. The imposter's home is saved and his or her credit history remains unblemished, while the victim suffers by having a bankruptcy filing remain on his or her credit reports for the next ten years. Later, the imposter can pose as the victim and transfer the title back into his or her name.

There have also been cases in which homeowners facing foreclosure or eviction transfer interest in their properties to victims who are currently petitioning for bankruptcy protection from lenders. Once the bankruptcy petitioner is listed as a partial owner, the bankruptcy case automatically forestalls foreclosure.

Victims of this kind of fraud must report it to the nearest U.S. Trustee field office, which will work with them to obtain the necessary information in order to pursue civil actions against the thief. (You can find a listing of regional field offices on the Department of Justice's Web site at http://www.usdoj.gov/ust or in the blue pages of your local phone directory.) Officials often recommend victims hire a lawyer to prove the bankruptcy filings were fraudulent and to clear their names.

Most people don't become aware they're victims of bankruptcy fraud until they notice the bankruptcy record on their credit reports or they receive a notice from the bankruptcy trustee, the court-appointed official who represents the interests of the lenders in a bankruptcy case.

MONEY ISN'T ALL THEY'RE AFTER

Not all identity thieves are after financial gain. As medical costs rise and health insurance coverage declines, an emerging area of identity theft is medical identity theft, which occurs when someone uses a person's name or insurance information to obtain medical treatment or drugs. Of course, there's a money angle, too, for the enterprising thief who poses as the victim to file false claims for insurance reimbursement. Often, victims discover the crime after receiving calls from collection agencies or when they discover their insurance-coverage limits have already been reached by an imposter.

Tracy Wright of Birmingham, Alabama, discovered he'd become a victim of medical identity theft after a collection agency contacted him about past-due medical bills. He later learned that an acquaintance had stolen his expired driver's license and then used it to impersonate him at a local hospital and run up more than $10,000 in medical bills. Luckily for Wright, the imposter's hand had been X-rayed when he was being treated for a dislocated thumb. That X-ray helped Wright, who had no such injury to his hand, ultimately clear his name.

Victims of medical identity theft sometimes discover that their medical records have been altered to include erroneous entries, the consequences of which can be grave. Victims in need of care may receive harmful treatments or medications based on incorrect information in their records. Or they may be turned down for a job because medical records indicate treatment for certain diseases or addictions that the victims never received.

And unlike victims of financial identity theft, medical identity-theft victims have limited protections under the law, according to a 2006 report from the World Privacy Forum entitled "Medical Identity Theft: The Information Crime That Can Kill You." The report estimates that about a quarter-million to a half-million individuals have become victims of this type of crime. Consumers by law have the right to review their own account statements, dispute charges and review credit reports to detect, protect and recover from financial identity theft. Under the Health Insurance Portability and Accountability Act, you have the right to review your medical records, though you may be charged a processing fee. If you discover fraudulent entries, ask your health-care provider to correct your records. Unfortunately, victims have no control over the flow of information in their files once fraudulent entries have been made, so even if health-care providers change erroneous information in their files, it's possible that the fraudulent entries may live on in other databases. And because many cases of medical identity theft have been found to have been perpetrated by individuals within the health-care community, victims could potentially be discussing their cases with the criminals themselves!

You can find out if someone has impersonated you to receive medical treatments by requesting in writing a listing of benefits paid in your name from your health insurer. If you discover payments made to health-care providers you don't recognize, contact your insurer's fraud department. You'll also need to contact the health-care provider and request that the fraudulent information be removed from your records. Some may balk at removing the information if you can't prove someone posed as you to obtain treatment. In this case, it may help to convince them to correct your records by filing a police report.

Another way to determine whether you've been a victim of medical identity theft is to check your Medical Information Bureau (MIB) report. The MIB is a group of six hundred companies involved in the insurance industry. When an underwriter at a member company has an applicant with a condition considered to be significant to his or her risk classification, that information is then reported on an MIB record. Life, health, disability or long-term care insurance companies use your MIB report the same way lenders use credit reports to help them gauge your creditworthiness. The information on your report is collected from health-care facilities and insurers. You can request the report by calling (866) 692-6901. If you discover information that doesn't belong in your file, you can dispute it with the bureau by writing to the MIB Information Office at MIB, Inc., P.O. Box 105, Essex Station, Boston, MA 02112. Unfortunately, if you haven't applied for individually underwritten life, health or disability insurance in the past seven years, the bureau won't have a record on you.

Finally, guard your health-care insurance card as carefully as you would your Social Security card. With it, thieves can obtain drugs and health-care services in your name, potentially limiting the amount of insurance you are entitled to.

FORGET THE KITCHEN SINK,
THEY TOOK THE WHOLE HOUSE!

If there's one thing you probably didn't think thieves could steal, it's your house. They might break into it, but steal the whole house? No way, you say.

Wrong!

No longer satisfied with the easy money to be had by opening fraudulent credit-card accounts, identity thieves now have their eyes on a much larger source of cash. Some homeowners have been astonished to find that thieves not only have stolen their personal information, but they've used it to open home-equity loans or, in some extreme cases, sold the homes to other people without the homeowners' knowledge. In one outrageous case, Stanley R. Miller of San Francisco used information he obtained on seventy-three-year-old Stanley E. Miller of Tinicum Township, Pennsylvania, to reroute the victim's mail to California. According to court papers, the thief then attempted to take ownership of the victim's house in order to sell it, and he even tried to convince a real-estate agent that the real homeowner was a trespassing squatter. Mr. Miller pleaded guilty to identity theft and a host of other felonies and was sentenced to probation for thirty-six months and required to pay $775 in restitution, according to the Bucks County Court clerk's office.

At first glance, home-equity theft may seem all but impossible to commit. Anyone who has attempted to obtain a home-equity loan or cash-out refinance knows the toil involved in collecting and copying reams of earnings and other financial documents for the application process. How could a thief such as Mr. Miller possibly steal that much information, let alone get away with passing himself off as a senior?

But the con is unnervingly easy to pull off, particularly when thieves take advantage of the boom in online lending. Many lenders typically allow the loan-application process to steam along by way of mail and fax, with the prospective borrower remaining sight unseen until the closing. By combining accurate financial information found online with forged or stolen documents to cover the rest, con artists can convince lenders they're the actual homeowner.

It's also easier to obtain a home-equity loan than it is to refinance, for example. Lenders typically don't require appraisals for loans that total less than 1 percent of the value of the home, and most home-equity loans don't require nearly as much documentation as does a mortgage.

Here's how a typical home-equity heist goes down. The thief looks for elderly homeowners who have only a few years left on their mortgages or have paid off their mortgages. Sometimes, the scammer will do some in-person reconnaissance by knocking on the door of the elderly victim and claiming to be a local real-estate agent working in the neighborhood. The con artist asks prying questions about the value of the home and whether the owner still holds a mortgage.

Once the criminal has harvested all the information he or she can get, he or she creates fraudulent documentation and uses it to apply for a home-equity loan in the victim's name. In some cases, the homes themselves are sold. In one scam, one criminal poses as a home buyer and applies for a mortgage to buy a home from the home seller, who's actually an identity thief posing as the homeowner. The "seller" then splits the mortgage money with the "buyer" and both vanish.

In another ruse, a con artist poses as a homeowner and sells a home to an unsuspecting person who is actually looking to buy a home. The identity thief takes the money and runs, and the real homeowners don't become aware of the scam until the new "owner" shows up to take possession of the property. Because the money is actually stolen from the lender, identity-theft victims aren't liable to repay the lost funds and don't lose their homes. It's the lender who is out of luck. But it takes time and considerable effort and expense to clear up the mess. Identity-theft experts say seniors are the most frequent target for this type of fraud, for two reasons: They tend to have accumulated more equity in their homes than younger homeowners, and they often are less aware of the need to guard it against identity theft.

THE METH CONNECTION

In June 2006, twenty-eight-year-old Jonathan Saatkamp pleaded no contest to charges of identity theft after admitting to stealing $16,000 from eleven victims, one a prominent Honolulu attorney. He was sentenced to fifteen years in prison. Mr. Saatkamp blamed his crime on his addiction to crystal methamphetamine, or meth.

Increasingly, law-enforcement officials are discovering the means of choice meth addicts use to feed their addiction is identity theft. Some have even turned it into big business: State and federal law enforcers broke up an identity-theft and meth ring in Georgia in July 2005 that turned up a laptop containing sixty-five thousand credit-card numbers, at least fourteen thousand of which were confirmed to be stolen.

While meth use isn't the only drug addiction that inspires identity theft, law-enforcement officials believe the drug's stimulating effects on its users—a hyperalert status that can last for hours—gives meth addicts plenty of time, as well as the mental concentration, to scrounge for bits of sensitive data in order to obtain all the information needed to open fraudulent lines of credit. The thieves then use those accounts to buy products, which they resell to raise cash to buy more meth or to make it.

It's believed that most meth abusers resort to extremely low-tech methods of obtaining data for use in identity theft. Indeed, in the Georgia bust, investigators said much of the personal data and financial-account information appeared to be stolen from trash bins and mailboxes—often snatched after residents left outgoing mail containing checks and other sensitive information in their mailboxes.

Meth addicts tend to operate on several levels. On the lowest rung are "collectors," users who sift through mailboxes, dumpsters or office trash bins for useful information. The collectors in turn sell their information to "converters"—the criminals who actually commit the theft by opening new accounts or making fraudulent online purchases. Authorities call thieves who buy the information from converters and then brazenly pass off fraudulent checks or credit cards in person "passers."

GIVING YOU A BAD NAME

While most identity fraud is aimed at getting money or goods, a new breed of identity thief isn't interested in money or even medical care. Instead, thieves want to impersonate you in order to shame or defame you, a particularly abhorrent use of personal data. It's most evident among young students, who create Web sites or enter chat rooms posing as other students. The imposters either use their target's stolen identity to say or do demeaning things that will get the target in trouble with friends or administrators, or they set up a fake Web site or Web logs (blogs) using the victim's image to tease or harass him or her.

But it's not just a kids' game. Gun statistics expert Dr. John Lott, a resident scholar at the American Enterprise Institute, was targeted in 2003 by an impersonator. A Google search of his name turned up a Web site called "AskJohnLott.org." On the site, visitors received a "Dear fellow gun owner" greeting and were encouraged to "Ask John Lott" any question about gun control. The problem was, Mr. Lott had nothing to do with the site. And worse, the imposter was using the Web site to attempt to discredit him by attributing statements to Lott that he would ideologically oppose. Among other things, the site falsely implied that Lott had reconsidered his support of the right of individuals to sell personally owned firearms to other individuals without government permission. Lott's attempts to get information on the bogus Web site removed were thwarted by the Internet service provider, who told him he'd have to get a criminal subpoena to find out who was running the Web site. Ultimately, Lott contacted a lawyer and eventually the site was taken down.

THE THIEF CHOOSES A VICTIM

The only more diverse group of people than identity thieves are their victims. Almost anyone is vulnerable to identity theft. Our lives require constant use of identity tools—credit cards, bank accounts, driver's licenses and Social Security numbers—and that data are stored in so many places and in so many forms that it is impossible for any of us to know with certainty who has access to our personal information and how it's being used. But studies of identity crime do indicate that some of us are more vulnerable than others, and particular age groups are more susceptible to certain types of theft than others.

It will probably unnerve you to learn that one of the fastest-growing target of identity thieves is children age eighteen or younger. Though they remain a very small portion of all identity-theft victims—just 4 percent of the total—the number of victims aged eighteen years or younger jumped more than 50 percent from 2003 to 2004, when there were almost ten thousand cases, according to the U.S. Federal Trade Commission. What's more disturbing is that the Identity Theft Resource Center, a San Diego consumer-advocacy group, estimates that more than half of all identity-theft cases involving children in 2004 were perpetrated by family members. In cases not involving family members, thieves who obtain children's dates of birth and Social Security numbers—through school and health-care records or sports-league applications—often use the information to fraudulently claim the child as a dependent on their tax returns.

Children can be victims of medical theft, too. Jonathan Brooks of Shoreline, Washington, discovered that his three-week-old son, Andrew, was the victim of identity theft in 2004 when a bill arrived in the mail from a local clinic. Someone had obtained baby Andrew's personal information and used it to buy prescription drugs.

Older children often learn that they have been victimized when they apply for their driver's license and discover that someone else has already applied for a license in their name. Red flags you should look for if you suspect your child has been a victim of identity theft include credit-card bills and other financial or medical statements addressed directly to the child.

FINANCIAL AID THEFT

A growing concern for high-school seniors is identity theft involving financial aid. John Christensen explained how he managed to game the system: He signed up for classes at a small community college in Arizona and used forty-three different stolen identities to collect more than $316,000 in federal financial aid and grants. Christensen would sign up for a class using stolen personal information and he would stay in the class for thirty days, the minimum amount of time needed to be eligible to receive the money. He's now in federal prison and tells his story in a U.S. Department of Education promotional video designed to educate college-aid officers about the growing problem.

Students often learn they've become victims when their aid package is turned down or when they can't get student loans because the thieves have already taken them out in the students' names and made off with the money. The problem is exacerbated because the pool of government funds available for financial aid is limited. John Christensen's thievery means that over $316,000 less aid is available to other students.

Students and parents not only have to be concerned about thieves stealing data directly from them, but they also have to worry about thieves obtaining it from their schools. A 2005 survey by ID Analytics of seventy data security breaches found that educational institutions accounted for the largest volume of data-breach incidents. (Financial services firms came in second.) Roughly 77 percent of the breaches consisted of data that were personally identifiable—names, addresses and Social Security numbers. The majority of the breaches weren't accidental: 70 percent were committed by individuals who specifically targeted the organization in an attempt to access the data.

Unfortunately, some colleges persist in the dangerously archaic practice of using students' Social Security numbers as college ID numbers. Colleges and universities that used to post student grades next to their names and student ID numbers on classroom walls are now posting them online, increasing the number of people who can potentially obtain the information to commit crimes.

THE COST OF CARELESSNESS

Men and women between the ages of eighteen and twenty-nine experienced the highest instances of identity-theft fraud in 2005, according to the FTC. This is in part because younger adults can be more careless than older workers and therefore are more likely to have their wallets and checkbooks lost or stolen, which is still the primary source of fraud involving personal information, as surveys done by Javelin Strategy & Research and the Better Business Bureau found. Younger adults may feel they're less likely to become victims of identity theft if they have relatively little in the way of finances, but as we've seen, thieves can use identities to create their own wealth. This age group also may be less aware of the dangers of giving out sensitive personal and financial information such as Social Security or bank-account numbers.

WHO'S MOST AT RISK?

This chart shows the individuals who are most at risk for becoming victims of identity fraud.

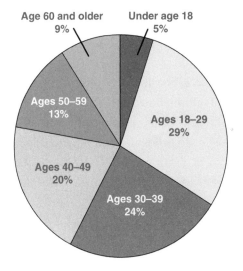

Source: Federal Trade Commission

The next group most at risk for identity theft is men and women in their thirties and forties, the FTC found. These individuals are most likely to be opening new lines of credit and using credit cards as they establish new families and buy new homes and cars. The more credit lines a person has open, the greater the opportunity for thieves to steal account information. Consumers in this group also are flooded with financial offers that often are cavalierly thrown in a trash can to become fodder for dumpster divers.

MEDICARE FRAUDSTERS

Surprisingly, seniors, most of whom are aged sixty or older, accounted for just 9 percent of all complaints to the FTC. But that's no reason for complacency. Crime rings have increasingly been targeting seniors, the age group that is most likely to benefit from government-assistance programs. In late 2005, a number of state attorneys general warned consumers of a scam involving the new Medicare prescription-drug program, in which thieves posed as door-to-door Medicare-authorized representatives and offered to help seniors fill out their Medicare forms for the drug-benefit program that began in January 2006. Victims unwittingly shared personal data, including their Medicare numbers, Social Security numbers, birth dates and other personal information that would allow con artists to pose as seniors to illegally tap government benefits.

One of the main problems seniors face is the many ways in which their Social Security numbers are available for the taking. Social Security numbers are used as identifiers on Medicare and veterans' benefits cards and on driver's licenses in a handful of states. In addition, some doctor and hospital medical bills and documents relating to retirement income also continue to include individuals' complete Social Security number, leaving seniors vulnerable to having the information stolen from their mailboxes before it's picked up or stolen from their garbage after the paperwork has been thrown away. A 2004 General Accounting Office report also warned that seniors must have their cards with them at the point of service, which increases the likelihood for accidental loss, theft or "shoulder surfing."

MAPPING IDENTITY THEFT

There's also a geographic connection to identity crime. Residents living in certain states and metropolitan areas are more at risk of becoming victims of identity theft than people living elsewhere. A look at the accompanying table shows the cities where identity theft is most likely to occur. The thieves are doing what the infamous British bank robber Willy Sutton did: They're going where the money is. The top-twenty places to be an identity thief are almost all large, prosperous metropolitan areas. Still, you might wonder what makes Arizona's main met-

WHERE THE THIEVES ARE

Do you live in an area at high risk of identity theft? Here are the Top 20 major metropolitan regions with the highest incidence of identity-theft-related consumer complaints in 2005.

Rank	Metropolitan Area	Complaints Per 100,000 Population
1	Phoenix-Mesa-Scottsdale, AZ	178.3
2	Las Vegas-Paradise, NV	158.5
3	Riverside-San Bernadino-Ontario, CA	145.7
4	Dallas-Fort Worth-Arlington, TX	141.2
5	Los Angeles-Long Beach-Santa Ana, CA	134.9
6	Miami-Ft. Lauderdale-Miami Beach, FL	131.7
7	San Francisco-Oakland-Fremont, CA	130.7
8	Houston-Baytown-Sugar Land, TX	128.1
9	San Diego-Carlsbad-San Marcos, CA	121.4
10	San Antonio, TX	119.1
11	Denver-Aurora, CO	117.5
12	Atlanta-Sandy Springs-Marietta, GA	117.5
13	Orlando, FL	115.6
14	Sacramento-Arden-Arcade-Roseville, CA	113.9
15	Seattle-Tacoma-Bellevue, WA	107.7
16	Washington-Arlington-Alexandria, D.C.-VA	107.2
17	Charlotte-Gastonia-Concord, NC-SC	104.2
18	San Jose-Sunnyvale-Santa Clara, CA	102.6
19	Chicago-Naperville-Joliet, IL	102.1
20	Austin-Round Rock, TX	100.8

Source: The Federal Trade Commission

ropolitan area a particularly attractive location for thieves. Law-enforcement officials attribute it to a combination of factors, not the least of which is that Maricopa County, which includes Phoenix, is among the fastest growing in the nation, with a continuing surge of wealthy retirees—many of whom live in planned communities with central mailboxes that offer

tempting targets to data thieves. Arizona is also a major desti-
nation for illegal immigrants looking for Social Security numbers and driver's licenses. Finally, the region has a growing
problem with methamphetamine users, and as we've already
seen, there's a strong connection between meth use and identity theft. Taken together, these contributing factors result in
identity theft that runs about twice the national average.

CHAPTER 3

VIGILANCE IS THE BEST PROTECTION

Now comes the hard part: setting up your defenses against all the bad apples who want to steal your identity. As I'm sure you're now well aware, there are so many ways that scamsters, tricksters and downright criminals can get your personal information that you might be tempted just to shrug and let fate take its course. But you don't have to give in. Although there's no guarantee that you won't become a victim—after all, one in thirty Americans already has suffered identity theft—there are numerous things that you can do to protect yourself by making it harder for the bad guys to get your data.

There are specific steps you should take. A lot of what you can do to defend yourself is simply a matter of training yourself to think like a data thief and then getting in the habit of taking appropriate defensive measures, such as using a shredder on any financial statements or pre-approved credit-card offers that a dumpster diver might use to steal your identity. In this chapter, we'll work through the various methods that everyone can use as defensive tactics, and then we'll look at steps that especially vulnerable groups can take. There will be some repetition, but that's okay. If you're like me, you'll benefit from being reminded a few times.

WHAT GOES OUT

The easiest way to begin protecting yourself from identity theft is to be sure you don't hand the thieves your personal data on a silver platter—or in a trash bag. Never let a piece of paper with any information that a thief could use leave your house in one piece. That obviously includes any financial or medical statements, but it also should apply to pre-approved credit-card offers and other solicitations. When you open a piece of mail, ask yourself right on the spot: Could this be useful to an identity thief? If the answer is even remotely "yes," shred it. Don't think of a good quality paper shredder as an expense, but as an investment, just like the locks on your doors. And make sure the shredder you buy is a "cross-cut" shredder, not the less expensive horizontal shredder, so thieves won't be able to piece the papers back together.

If you think thieves can't be bothered piecing torn-up statements together, think again. There's a reason you've been hearing more about the increasing problem of methamphetamine users resorting to identity theft—law-enforcement officials say the drug creates a sense of focused attention and heightened alertness that likes nothing better than the challenge of reassembling a few hundred strips of paper to discover a credit-card or Social Security number.

Disposing of paperwork away from home is another habit you'll need to break. It may clutter up your wallet or your purse to hang on to receipts and other paperwork that bears your personal stamp, but it's worth it to haul that stuff home and turn it into shredded mulch. That way you know somebody searching through the shopping center or airport dumpsters—or your garbage at work—won't find his or her way into your bank account.

Putting something in the mail is another source of potential danger. When you pay bills with checks and then place the envelopes in your mailbox for your friendly mail carrier to pick up later in the day, you're offering an identity thief a welcome cash infusion. All he or she has to do is arrive ahead of the mail carrier and lift your waiting mail, take it home, use acetone to erase the payee's name and use his or her own pen to make the check out to himself or herself. Street-side mailboxes—the kind the mail carrier can reach without leaving his or her vehicle—are more vulnerable than mailboxes on the front porch, but brazen thieves have little trepidation about hiking from one house to another, especially in neighborhoods with working couples who are likely to be away from home most of the day. The good news is that it is fairly easy to protect yourself: Get a locking mailbox for which only you have the key. Especially for outgoing mail with sensitive information, hang on to it until you're making a grocery run, and then drop it in a U.S. Postal Service box.

WHAT COMES IN

Incoming mail is just as vulnerable as outgoing, especially when you receive a new credit card or a new box of checks from your bank. Again, a locking mailbox is the obvious solution, but a post office box, while somewhat inconvenient, offers good protection, too. You can also learn your mail carrier's routine and get to the box to retrieve your mail as soon as he or she drops it off.

More importantly, though, you can reduce your vulnerability to identity theft by tackling the problem at the source and reducing the amount of mail you receive. To stem the tide of credit offers pouring into your mailbox, you can opt out of receiving the solicitations by calling (888) 5OPTOUT. The information you provide will be sent to all of the major marketing agencies telling them to remove your information from their pre-approved credit offer lists. You'll be asked by a recorded message to provide, among other information, your Social Security number, as a means to identify you. Don't let it spook you; the service is secure. The opt-out is good for two years before it expires, so mark your calendar. You can also go to the Direct Marketing Association's Web site at www. dmaconsumers.org/privacy.html to set your preferences for the kinds of offers you don't want to receive in the mail. Just remember that this won't stop offers coming to you from companies you already do business with. You'll have to notify those businesses to take you off their mailing lists yourself under the terms of their privacy policies.

Many financial institutions would prefer to communicate with you online rather than preparing and mailing statements. Take them up on that offer. It's good for you because it's one less way in which thieves can get at your personal data and it's good for them because it saves postage and printing costs. If you insist on receiving paper statements in the mail, jot down on your calendar when you expect to receive those statements. If the statements are more than a few days late, contact the sender to determine if there was some unexpected delay in preparing and mailing the statements. If the company says the statements are being sent to a new address, that's a red flag that you've become a victim. Have the statements rerouted to your house, and then immediately request a copy of your credit report (more about ordering and understanding your credit report later) to check for other signs that you may be a victim of identity theft.

Do you have more than two credit cards? Why? If you don't need them all, ditch as many as you can. The more credit-card statements coming to you and bills being paid by you, the better the chance that a thief can get his or her hands on one. (Cut the credit cards up, but if you've had the credit-card accounts for many years don't close the account—closing a bunch of accounts with a long history of on-time payments may lower your credit score.) Keep one or two cards that have the best rates and the longest credit histories to minimize the temporary dent to your credit score, which is based in part on the length of time you've been borrowing. Two credit cards are useful because you can use one exclusively for online transactions and the other for over-the-counter purchases. That way, if something goes wrong and your credit card is used fraudulently, you'll be better able to track down the source of the problem or cancel the card without being cardless. If you need an array of credit cards because you keep maxing them out, then you've got problems that go beyond identity theft and probably need to get your financial house in order.

To prevent a thief from opening an account without your permission, place a "fraud alert" on file with the three major credit-reporting agencies. The fraud alert requires creditors to provide proof of identity and then alerts you that a request for credit has been made in your name before the account can be opened.

There are pros and cons to placing a fraud alert on your account: On the plus side, you have one more barrier in place to try to thwart an identity thief before a fraudulent account is opened in your name. Unfortunately, though, borrowers must remember to contact the credit-reporting companies and pay a fee to cancel the alerts temporarily before they apply for credit. Still, I think the pluses outweigh the minuses, particularly if you suspect you may be a victim of fraud. To place a fraud alert, contact each of the three major credit-reporting agencies and request that a fraud alert be placed on your files.

Equifax
P.O. Box 740250
Atlanta, GA 30374
(800) 525-6285

Experian
P.O. Box 1017
Allen, TX 75013
(888) 397-3742

TransUnion
P.O. Box 6790
Fullerton, CA 92634
(800) 680-7289

Once you've requested that a fraud alert be placed on your files, ask that the reporting agencies confirm your request in writing and send you a free copy of your credit report. Having a fraud alert on your credit report doesn't affect your credit score, but depending on your credit history lenders may see the alert as a negative factor when considering whether to extend you credit. For this reason, be sure to have the fraud alert removed from all three credit reports before applying for credit. And don't become complacent! Consumer watchdogs tell me that fraud alerts aren't foolproof—some businesses do a shoddy job of verifying proof of identity and others ignore fraud alerts entirely. So you'll need to continue to monitor your credit reports for any signs of suspicious activity. (I'll show you how when we tackle credit reports in Chapter 4.)

STRONG PROTECTION, EARLY DETECTION

Okay, we've taken steps to keep the thieves from finding our personal data in trash cans or through the mail we send and receive. There are other cautionary steps we can take to prevent data theft, particularly for the most sensitive financial information. If you're thinking like a thief, you already know you don't leave your checkbook in the car while you run into the grocery store for a gallon of milk. But you shouldn't leave it on your desk at work, either, or even in a desk drawer unless it's locked. Ditto with deposit slips or financial statements. Even when you're home, such information should be secured out of sight of the prying eyes of friends and family members, house cleaners, laborers or anyone else who has access to your home (remember, much of identity theft is done by people known to the victims). Boxes of blank checks should be kept in a secure location. To avoid being caught, thieves often steal a check or three from an open checkbook, hoping the victim won't notice the jump in sequential order of the checks.

Prevention is the best defense, but it's also important to find out as quickly as possible when your data has been compromised. Between bank savings, checking accounts, credit-card accounts and investment accounts, it can be downright tough to keep a constant eye on the ebb and flow of your financial life. But monitoring your financial accounts on a regular basis is crucial to beating identity theft. One day, you might see a credit-card charge that you can't quite remember making, or a check suddenly shows up on your bank account that you know you didn't write. A quick call to your financial institution's toll-free emergency hotline and bingo! You've uncovered a theft early and will likely avoid having to pay for the charge yourself. If months have gone by before you notice a questionable charge on one of your credit-card accounts, you may get stuck paying for it.

Thankfully, technology has made it easy to monitor financial accounts. Most financial institutions offer online access, where you can view up-to-the-minute transactions and stay on top of your accounts. Set aside a few minutes every day to take a quick look at all your financial accounts to ensure no fraudulent transactions slip through.

DEFENDING THE NUMBER

There are lots of numbers in our lives these days, but the only one that is likely to follow us from cradle to grave is our Social Security number. Without it, we're nothing, at least according to the government. That's why some people are so eager to steal it and why we need to be especially protective of it.

Introduced in 1935 for the sole purpose of helping the government keep track of Social Security retirement accounts, the number has experienced a form of mission creep. By the early 1960s, the IRS was using the number as an individual taxpayer identifier, and employers, banks and other institutions that have to report to the IRS were required by the agency to begin requesting the information. The military, colleges and universities, and health-care providers also adopted the numbers as a way to identify individuals. And companies that require Social Security numbers in order to pay payroll taxes often use the number as in-house ID numbers. Creditors routinely collect the numbers in order to gain access to applicants' credit histories.

Other private-sector companies have no legal right to the number, but there's no law against asking for it. Unaware of the danger, many people readily comply. It wasn't so long ago that people were printing their Social Security numbers on their checks to save time at the checkout counter!

Today there is a mishmash of federal and state laws and regulations that restrict how your Social Security number can be used. Generally, any government agency that has been using Social Security numbers prior to 1975—the year the Privacy Act of 1974 went into effect—has the right to demand your Social Security number. Other state and local organizations are also permitted to request the number under the Privacy Act, including the Department of Motor Vehicles, state and local welfare organizations and the tax man. Under the law, however, you are entitled to receive a disclosure statement that explains, in part, why the agency is asking for the information and how it will be used.

Fortunately, many big employers, universities and health insurers have changed their policies in recent years and abandoned Social Security numbers as identifiers in response to consumer-watchdog groups' outcries over privacy concerns. If your employer or health-insurance company still uses your Social Security number to identify you, explain your objections in writing and request that the policy be changed. There's one exception: If you're seeking credit, it's unlikely you'll be able to obtain it unless you divulge your Social Security number. If you don't provide your Social Security number, expect to be charged sky-high rates that are assigned to the riskiest category of borrowers.

So how do you guard your Social Security number closely? First, get your Social Security card out of your wallet and into a secure, locked firebox along with all your other sensitive financial and personal documents, including birth certificates, passports, military documents and marriage licenses. If your company requires you to carry an identification card that has your Social Security number on it, ask if you can obtain an ID with a different number.

Among the companies and organizations that continue to routinely ask for your Social Security number, even though some don't need it, are health-care providers, life insurers, retailers, video rental stores, utilities, health clubs, universities and blood banks. Typically, if you strongly object to offering up your Social Security number, many will find alternate means to identify you.

If you do decide to divulge your Social Security number to a private company, or if you have in the past, be sure to ask about the company's privacy policy. You should have the right to opt out of allowing the company to share your information, even among its own entities. Once you opt out, keep an eye on your mail: You may have to opt out on an annual basis.

Protecting yourself from the criminal use of your Social Security number isn't easy. It's unlikely you'll know right away that someone is using your Social Security number to obtain work unless the thief used the number to open financial accounts in your name or to commit other crimes. Check your Social Security Earnings Record at www.ssa.gov/mystatement or request a copy at (800) 772-1213. If your statement indicates that you are earning more than you do, contact the Social Security Administration to report potential fraud.

If your Social Security number has been compromised, under certain circumstances you may be able to get a new one. (To learn more, visit the Social Security Administration's Web site at www.ssa.gov.) Generally, though, obtaining a new Social

Security number causes more headaches for a victim than it solves: By obtaining a new number, you become a new borrower with no credit history, sending your credit score into the basement. And, since you're entering the equivalent of a witness-protection program, it can raise suspicion among creditors, insurers, landlords and employers, who sometimes rely on credit reports to gauge your financial stability.

IDENTITY THEFT-PROOFING YOUR CHILD

I bet you were as shocked as I was to find out that the theft of children's identities is the fastest-growing form of identity crime. To protect your children, you need to monitor their personal information—and the companies they do business with—as closely as you monitor your own. Most kids spend a lot of time online these days. We'll delve more deeply into computer security later, but you should be aware that the Children's Online Privacy Act regulates the collection of data on children under age thirteen. The act also gives parents more control over how companies use their children's information.

Your children's personal documents—Social Security card, birth certificate and other sensitive information—should be in the lockbox with your documents. Avoid giving out sensitive information when at all possible, such as to sports leagues and health-care providers. An unsolicited offer of credit or other services in your child's name should be an instant red flag. Request a free copy of the child's credit report immediately and review it for any evidence of identity theft. Carefully review the privacy policy statements of any Web site directed at your child to find out what types of data are being collected, how they will be used and whether they will be shared with any other business or organization. Finally, if you suspect your child's data are being used improperly, contact the site's operators and revoke your permission to use your child's personal information. Then, attempt to obtain a copy of your child's credit report for signs of illegal activity.

You may recall that in an earlier chapter, I mentioned the increasingly insidious form of identity theft involving children that has begun to crop up on social-networking Web sites such as Facebook, Friendster and MySpace. Malicious students create fake Web logs, or blogs—electronic diaries that publicly share intimate details about such things as schoolyard crushes or feuds along with pictures and audio files. The child then poses as another child, often posting hateful or malicious information about the victim. The victimized children often find the public humiliation devastating. In cases such as these, parents should contact the site's administrators as soon as possible and request to have the offending page removed. Most sites will comply without requiring proof that the page is a fake.

As they get older, kids typically get new privileges, such as a driver's license and perhaps their own credit cards (with strict limits on spending, if you're smart). Given their tendency toward carelessness, it's particularly important that teens carry only one credit card and that statements for that card be sent to the parents' address so that they can monitor it for unusual charges that might indicate illegal use of the card (or unfettered use by the children).

It's not a bad idea to request that a fraud alert be placed on a child's files—just remember that it's not a foolproof defense and that you'll need to call and have the alert temporarily removed if and when your child does apply for credit. Just as you have a good paper shredder in your den or home office, your kid in college should have one in the dorm room and be told to use it. Your child's checkbook should never be left lying around the dorm room or apartment, and he or she should be cautioned to never share financial-account information, including PINs and passwords, with friends or roommates. PINs shouldn't be obvious numbers, such as birth dates or any part of your child's Social Security number. And if the school student ID number is your child's Social Security number, you and other concerned parents should organize a campaign to get the school's administrators to catch up with the rest of the world and use some other means to identify students.

SENIOR SECURITY

Seniors are often the target of hard-sell routines. Some become inured to such tactics and don't think twice about slamming down the receiver on a caller or shutting the door in the face of a salesperson. But many seniors grew up in more formal and polite times and don't always forcefully assert their rights to privacy. If you're in this category, keep in mind that you can politely refuse to give your Social Security number, account number, password or any other identifying information to people who call you requesting it, and refusing to give in to requests is particularly important with callers who badger you or try to intimidate you. Your security depends on your resolve. Hang up and call the organization back to determine whether the caller was a legitimate representative of the company. If he or she was, let the company know in no uncertain terms that you don't appreciate such harassment and will hold it against the company if it happens again.

Many generous seniors give willingly to a range of charities. But be selective in your giving and carefully screen requests for charity at Web sites such as www.charitywatch.org. When you do give, send a letter requesting that your information isn't shared with other parties. Further, I advise taking a pass on any sweepstakes. The odds are long enough anyway, but too many of them ask you to provide a wealth of personal information that identity thieves can easily use to impersonate you.

If you're worried about forgetting to be as vigilant as you should, you can make things easier on yourself by enlisting a trusted child—I emphasize the word "trusted"—to keep an eye on financial accounts and remind you to check your credit reports for fraudulent activity a few times a year.

USING TECHNOLOGY WISELY

I'll get into some of the more sophisticated ways identity thieves work the Internet to get at your sensitive data later in a chapter that those of you who aren't *technorati* may find a little daunting. But there are enough of us online who don't completely understand computers, the Internet and other digital data products and services that it's worth taking a few minutes to look at some routine protective measures we all need to take, realizing that high-tech thieves are working 24/7 to steal personal information.

While online identity theft may not be the most common way thieves steal account and other sensitive information, it's still a very real threat. The reason? You make it so easy! By leaving your personal computer and online accounts poorly protected, identity thieves can easily grab the information they need to empty your financial accounts or open new ones.

Let's start with your personal computer. To discourage hackers from targeting your PC, install firewall software—a virtual door that's designed to prevent unauthorized access to or from your computer. I say "discourage" because even the most optimistic software makers admit that it's next to impossible to stop a technology-savvy thief from breaking into your computer. But installing a firewall can prove to be a deterrent—why spend the time breaking into a firewall-protected computer when there are so many computers out there without the software?

Next, pay closer attention to how you do business online, starting with the Web sites you visit. If you intend to do any financial transaction on a Web site, make sure it's a legitimate and secure site. You can check to make sure a company is a legitimate business on sites such as the Better Business Bureau (www.bbbonline.org) and TRUSTe (www.truste.com). Also check to make sure it's a "secure site"—a secure Web site has a Web address (or URL) that starts with "https://" instead of "http://." These sites tend to use a form of technology known as Secure Sockets Layer (SSL) that encrypts data, which makes it tougher for hackers to access.

Another indicator of a secure site is the VeriSign Secured™ Seal. VeriSign provides SSL encryption and authentication services for most major businesses. (Note that entire Web sites, including security seals, can be copied by crafty identity thieves, but the splash identification page that pops up when a user clicks the seal adds an extra layer of legitimacy.) You can find the seal and a search engine to verify that a Web site is legitimate at VeriSign's Web site (http://www.verisignsecured.com/). Finally, check for the lock icon that should appear in the lower-right corner of your browser window. That lock, whether open or closed, lets you know whether the Web site is protected by encryption. A closed lock means it is, while an open lock indicates it isn't. (A broken lock indicates some elements of the site are encrypted, while some aren't.) Finally, depending on your Web browser, some sites will display a closed lock icon directly adjacent to the Web address, which indicates that the site is encrypted.

Using all of these methods can help you to spot fraudulent sites, but remember that Web bandits are always working to find ways around these safeguards. If you have any doubts about a Web site's authenticity, err on the side of caution and don't provide personal information or make a financial transaction.

Next, pay attention to your account passwords. In the 1994 Harrison Ford movie *Clear and Present Danger,* it takes a CIA computer technician seconds to figure out an agent's password—a combination of the birth dates of various family members. The truth is, most people choose passwords that are extremely simple to guess. Easy-to-crack passwords often include a loved one's name, maiden name, or birth date; the last four digits of one's Social Security number; a pet's name; or consecutive numbers.

So what's the recipe for a secure password? Use acronyms, not the actual words or names, and wherever possible, replace letters with numbers or symbols that correlate (the @ sign for the letter "a," zero for the letter "o," one for the letters "i" or "l" or "s" for the number five). Make the password memorable by choosing something that's memorable to you—maybe your favorite movie or song, but not something that other people can find out about you with a quick Google search. For example, if you're a big Stephen King fan, combine the first letters of his name with his short story "Rita Hayworth and the Shawshank Redemption" and you get "skrhatsr." Now swap the "s" for the number five and the letter "a" for the @, and you get 5krh@t5r.

Then give each of your high-value online accounts a unique password, so that a thief can't gain access to all of your financial accounts by obtaining the password to just one. An easy way to do this is to add an additional few letters to identify the site: For a credit-card account, tack on a "cc" to your password to get 5krh@t5rcc. Then mark your calendar to remind yourself to change the passwords every two or three months.

Finally, when the time comes to upgrade your computer, don't just toss your old one in the garbage or simply give it away without eliminating all of the sensitive information stored on it. Simply sending your files to the recycling bin isn't enough, because the information can be recovered by a thief. Instead, buy a data "wipe" utility program. This software completely eliminates data from your computer so that they can't be recovered. I have a friend who takes his old computers with him on saltwater fishing trips and tosses them overboard in two hundred feet of water. While I don't suggest you follow suit, even if some scuba diver stumbles across one, the salt water has destroyed the drives and other electrical components.

A PLAN FOR PASSWORD SLACKERS

If you just can't cope with managing or remembering numerous passwords, at the very least make sure none of your high-value passwords are used in low-value situations. For example, don't use the same password that unlocks your credit-card account to sign up for your favorite online message board. For high-value sites, take the time to create, memorize and regularly update your passwords. But for low-value situations, figure out some kind of scheme that will let you use a different but easily remembered password in each case—perhaps one that incorporates the name of the Web site, such as wa11str3tj0urnal. It's not ideal, but it's a start.

Here are a few more tech tips:

- Never store financial account or password information on your workplace computer, and avoid using workplace e-mail to send any information that could expose you to identity thieves. When in doubt, delete all your "cookies," which are programs that are automatically downloaded onto users' computers and can store information about your identity and Web surfing habits.

- Don't go phishing. That means never responding to official-looking e-mails from companies you do business with requesting your Social Security number, personal account information or passwords. No legitimate company would ever request such information from you online.

- Take advantage of any offer from your credit-card issuer for the use of "virtual credit-card numbers" to provide additional protection when shopping online. The companies will generate a substitute card number for every online purchase so that your real card number is never accessed by the retailer or service.

- Sign up for e-mail alerts from banks and credit-card companies that notify you when suspicious transfers are made, low balances are detected or any of your contact information is changed. Many banks and card issuers have their own fraud-prevention technologies and will contact customers on their own if they suspect fraudulent activity, but don't rely on them to catch thefts 100 percent of the time.

- Memorize your passwords, and don't write them down unless you intend on keeping the information under lock and key. If a Web site offers you the option of saving your password for future use, don't go for it. High-tech data-recovery methods make permanently deleting data stored on your computer's hard drive difficult. Saving your password is the equivalent of allowing anyone who will ever use your computer—both now and after you've moved on to a newer model—to share your account and password information.

- If your account passwords or PINs are blocked by your lender or are not working properly, your financial institution may have suspected fraud and changed the passwords for your own protection—or an identity thief may have changed them. Contact your bank, broker, credit union or lender immediately.

- If someone claiming to represent a legitimate business calls or e-mails and asks for your password or PIN, don't provide it. Contact the business's 800 number directly or type the Web address into your Internet browser on your own and inform customer service about the attempt to steal your information.

KEEPING UP WITH THE THIEVES

You may recall that in Chapter 2 I discussed some of the more innovative ways in which thieves are using identities, including bankruptcy fraud, medical theft and even outright theft of people's homes. When it comes to innovative identity theft, the preventive measures aren't always as clear as we would want—at least not yet. Still, don't give up hope. Here are some ways to protect yourself from these clever criminals.

UTILITY THEFT

When terminating electric, gas, telephone, cell phone, Internet and all other types of utility contracts, be sure to do so in writing and ask the company to verify that no other accounts exist in your name. Follow up a few weeks later to ensure that all services in your name have been turned off.

EMPLOYMENT IDENTITY THEFT

Job seekers need to be extra vigilant about protecting their identity, both online and off. Before posting your résumé on a job-search Web site, check the company's privacy policy to find out how your information may be used and whether you can quickly have your résumé removed at your request. Never include your home address, work phone number, date of birth or—as you know by now—Social Security number on your résumé. And if you're searching for a job through reputable Web sites such as Monster.com or CareerBuilder.com, take advantage of identity-suppression features that allow you to post your résumé anonymously.

If you're contacted by someone who says he or she has been asked by an employer to do a background check on you, get his or her telephone number and tell the person you'll have to call back. Before calling back, check with the Better Business Bureau to ensure that the company or background-check firm is legitimate. Then follow up with a phone call to the company to make sure it is on the up-and-up. If you're receiving a lot of bogus job offers as a result of posting your résumé online, you can set up phony e-mail accounts to receive incoming job offers and make use of any spam-filtering tools to ensure a legitimate job inquiry doesn't get lost in the junk mail.

Finally, don't offer any personal information about yourself until the company actually makes you a job offer, and then inquire how the company secures that information once it's provided. And enjoy your new position!

MEDICAL IDENTITY THEFT

This type of theft tends to fall under the heading of thefts you want to find out about quickly—rather than preventing—since it can be difficult to head off this kind of thief. Start by avoiding anyone claiming to be affiliated with Medicare who sells products or offers to enroll you in a drug plan. You can find information and assistance on how to choose and enroll in Medicare drug programs by checking online at www.medicare.gov or calling (800) MEDICARE. If you feel you may have been scammed, contact Medicare immediately at (800) 633-4227.

You should request a statement from your insurer once a year, detailing all benefits paid out for the year. If you see any payouts that are suspicious, contact your insurer and dispute the claim. Also ask your insurer to verify your current address to ensure that an imposter hasn't used your information to change your billing address. You are also entitled under the Health Insurance Portability and Accountability Act to an "accounting of disclosures" from your health insurer or healthcare provider (note that you may be charged a small fee to copy the records and postage if you request to have the documents mailed to your home). The accounting spells out who was given access to your personal records and for what purpose.

You also have the right under federal law to receive a copy of your medical records from your health-care provider, though again you'll likely be charged a small fee. (See sample request letter in the appendix.) By law, the health-care provider has up to thirty days to respond to your request (the provider can have an additional thirty days if it can document good cause). Many states have enacted their own health privacy laws that govern how much health-care providers can charge and how much time they have to respond to patient requests for records. The Georgetown University Center on Medical Rights and Privacy has compiled a list of thirty-two state guides to help consumers understand their rights. It can be found online at http://hpi.georgetown.edu/privacy/records. html.

After reviewing your records, be sure to keep them in a secure place, as these documents generally include Social Security number, date of birth, insurance records and other extremely sensitive personal information. If you spot any errors or treatments you never received, you may have trouble getting the information removed from your file. Often, however, you can request that the file be amended to include a statement from you that disputes the erroneous information—including any evidence you have to back up your complaint.

HOME-EQUITY THEFT

It still stuns me to think that some clever identity thief could steal my home equity! Because home-equity theft is so unexpected, it's important for homeowners to keep their guard up for suspicious signs that may prompt them to check their credit reports. Look for unusual mailings that appear to be from lenders or others requesting financial information. If you get a phone call from a person claiming to be from a company with whom you do business and asking for sensitive personal information such as your Social Security number, hang up— it's likely a scam. And be swift to end conversations with "door-to-door Realtors" who seem to be asking for a little too much detail about what you owe and to whom.

One unusual red flag is a visit from Welcome Wagon. This Westbury, New York, company uses home sales data to find new homeowners and welcomes them to their new homes with small gifts—along with ads and coupons from local businesses and services. If you've lived in a home for a long time and suddenly receive a Welcome Wagon package for the "new owner," it could be a sign that your house has been fraudulently sold.

Finally, be sure your parents or elderly relatives, since the elderly are most often victims of this and other identity-theft crimes, are aware of the scams. Encourage them to check their own credit reports regularly (as we will learn in the next chapter) and be vigilant about protecting their personal information.

CHAPTER 4

THE VITAL DOCUMENT:
YOUR CREDIT REPORT

There are many things it isn't. It isn't pretty. It isn't well-written. It isn't even always very accurate. But for all that it isn't, your credit report *is* the single most important document for protecting yourself from identity theft.

What makes a simple document so valuable?

It's a record of your financial life. No other document contains as much financial information about you—and your borrowing and spending habits—as your credit report. Your credit report includes your name (and any other name you've borrowed credit under over the course of your lifetime), your Social Security number, current and past addresses and phone numbers and current and former employers. It also tracks every account opening and closing, every late payment and every dime you borrow.

HOW A CREDIT REPORT IS COMPILED

Most credit reports are compiled by three companies known generically as "credit bureaus": Equifax in Atlanta, Georgia (www.equifax.com); Experian of Allen, Texas (www.experian.com); and TransUnion Corp. of Chicago, Illinois (www.transunion.

com). These three agencies are in a kind of symbiotic relationship with almost every business that grants credit to consumers. When you apply for credit from a bank or credit-card issuer, the information you provide about your financial situation along with the amount of the loan you're requesting and the size of your monthly payments is sent by the financial institution to the three credit bureaus. What's more, the bank or credit-card company sends the three bureaus updated information each month, noting, for instance, whether your scheduled payment was late or wasn't made at all. In return for providing all that information, the bank or credit-card company can, for a fee, obtain the credit reports of anyone else applying to them for a loan or credit card. They then use the credit report to determine if the applicant should get a loan and, if so, what interest rate should be charged given the individual's repayment history with other lenders. A bank will first use your credit report to determine if you get a loan and then will report on how well you keep up with payments so that future lenders will know whether to loan you money.

But it isn't just lenders delving into your file. Other businesses have discovered that your borrowing habits say a lot about you as a person. Employee recruiters have added credit reports to the list of background checks they perform. Auto- and health-insurance companies want to see how much risk you take with your finances before they risk insuring you. And landlords not only check credit reports to ensure tenants tend to pay their bills on time, they're leaving negative information on the credit reports of renters who skip out without paying what they owe.

To make it easier to determine if you should get a loan, the information contained in your credit report is quantified and becomes a single number, called your "credit score." For a long time, the only provider of credit scores was a company called Fair Isaac Corporation (FICO) in Minneapolis, Minnesota. Lately, however, the three credit bureaus have banded together to compete against Fair Isaac and offer lenders another version of the credit score. I'll explain more about credit scoring later.

As important as credit reports are to our financial lives, it's surprising that the information contained in them sometimes differs from one bureau to another. For example, a delinquent payment on an old student loan might show up on a report from Experian, but not on reports issued by Equifax or Trans-Union. Worse, credit reports often contain errors. Although the credit bureaus dispute the findings, a 2004 study by the National Association of State Public Interest Research Groups found that 79 percent of credit reports—four out of five—in a survey of two hundred people contained one or more errors. An estimated 25 percent of those errors were serious enough to result in a denial of credit, insurance or even a job. I think you're beginning to see why it's important to get familiar with your credit report.

INTERPRETING YOUR CREDIT REPORT

Only a few years ago, figuring out what all the gibberish on your credit report meant required the equivalent of a degree in finance—or the ability to read ancient hieroglyphics. But recently, the reports have become a lot more consumer-friendly, as credit-reporting agencies came under pressure from government agencies and consumer-advocacy groups to make the files easier to understand.

Today's credit reports are broken down into four basic sections: information that identifies you, your borrowing history, any public records available and the types of companies that have requested information about your file. (For an example of a good, a bad and an average credit report—and how to read each—see the case study at the end of this chapter.)

Section one includes information specific to you. It's very common to find errors—and occasionally fraudulent information—in this section. Don't panic: It's common to find that your name has been misspelled or that many variations of your name appear. Credit-reporting companies rely on information provided by your creditors, and often something gets lost in the translation. Other information might include your current and previous addresses, your date of birth, telephone numbers, driver's license numbers and your employer's and your spouse's name. When there is cause for alarm is when you discover an entirely different name, address or driver's license number on your file. These are a few red flags for possible identity theft.

Next comes your credit history. Here you'll find a line-by-line description of every creditor account that has been reported to the agency. These entries include

- the name of the lender and account number;

- when the account was opened;

- whether it is an installment account (say, car loan) or a revolving account (such as a credit card);

- whether the account was opened with another person;

- the account's credit limit and your outstanding balance;

- the size of the monthly payment;

- whether the account is still open, and if not, who closed it;

- the number of delinquencies on the account; and

- whether the account went into collection or was written off by the creditor.

This is where you'll want to spend some time looking over the information carefully. For example, people with very common surnames (the Smiths, the Jones, and the Cullens for that matter) frequently find that someone else's account information

WHOOPS!

When my husband and I purchased our first home back in 1992, I'll never forget the look on his face when our mortgage broker presented him with a credit report that read like a criminal rap sheet. The report was littered with past-due accounts he'd never opened and included all of his father's credit lines as well. Some of the accounts were opened in the early 1960s—before he was born! Turns out Cullen is the "Smith" of Ireland, and many delinquent borrowers share my husband's (and his father's and my son's) first name.

Errors such as these abound in individual credit reports, according to a 2004 study by the National Association of State Public Interest Research Groups (PIRG). The group collected two hundred surveys from adults in thirty states who reviewed their credit reports for accuracy. Here's a rundown on some of the most-common mistakes found:

- 79 percent of the credit reports contained mistakes of some kind.

- 54 percent contained personal demographic identifying information that was misspelled, long-outdated, belonged to a stranger or was otherwise incorrect.

- 30 percent contained credit accounts that had been closed by the consumer but incorrectly remained listed as open.

- 25 percent contained errors such as erroneous public records that were serious enough to result in the denial of credit.

appears on their credit report. It happens most often within families—a father's mortgage might appear on his college-aged son's credit report because they share the same name. If you find information that's inaccurate, notify the agency immediately using the dispute form that accompanies your credit report in the mail.

While most people believe the borrowing-history contains the information that is most harmful to your credit score, the real damage happens in the next section: public records. Here you'll find public filings on such things as past judgments, liens and bankruptcy protection filings. If you've ever been convicted of a criminal activity, such as drunk driving or drug use, your record very well might show up here, too.

Finally, the "inquiries" section lists the types of companies that have requested information about you. There are two types of inquiries: hard and soft. Whenever you do such things as request a copy of your own credit report, apply for a credit card or sign up for a new cell phone plan, it's considered a hard inquiry. Soft inquiries, on the other hand, are initiated by companies that want to sell you something, such as a new rewards credit card or pre-approved line of credit.

The number of inquiries is factored into the formula that determines your credit score—a large number is seen as a negative, in that you may be taking on too much credit. But scoring companies understand that consumers may need to make a number of inquiries in a short span of time when shopping for mortgages or car loans, and they factor that into the scoring accordingly.

CORRECTING
CREDIT REPORT ERRORS

To dispute a claim, you need to create a paper trail: Keep copies of all documents you send or receive from the credit agency or the lender and the names and phone numbers of people who contacted you about your dispute (and their supervisor's name). Contact the credit-reporting agency and the lender who provided the inaccurate information (if it's clear where the bad information came from) to dispute the claim in writing—using the sample letter provided in Appendix 1. Send it certified mail so you have proof the dispute was sent. You can also dispute the error online on the Web sites of the three

CREDIT-MONITORING SERVICES

Here is a sampling of some credit-monitoring companies, their costs and some of the services they provide. Credit-reporting companies offer services that monitor their own credit reports, or you can subscribe to services that monitor reports from all three credit-reporting companies.

Single-Report Companies

EQUIFAX

$9.95/month; unlimited access to credit report

Provides daily e-mail alerts within twenty-four hours for account and personal information changes, credit inquiries, changes to existing accounts and any new accounts or public records added.

EXPERIAN

$9.95/month; quarterly access to credit report

Provides daily alerts via e-mail, phone or text messaging for account and personal information changes, credit inquiries, new accounts or negative information added.

TRUECREDIT
(a service of TransUnion and Lehman Brothers)

Free for thirty days, then $9.95 a month; unlimited access to credit report and score

Free credit score and debt analysis; weekly e-mail alerts for credit inquiries, account and personal information changes, new accounts and public records added and any improvement in the credit score.

Multiple-Report Companies

CITI

$9.95/month (first month free); reports can be ordered online once every thirty days

A three-in-one credit report with data from Equifax, Experian and TransUnion, along with credit scores; daily alerts by e-mail, phone and text messaging notifying one of personal information changes, credit inquiries, changes to existing accounts and any new accounts or public records added; free credit analysis and identity-theft insurance up to $25,000.

IDENTITY GUARD

$25.95/month for three months, $12.99/month thereafter; quarterly access to credit reports and credit score

A three-in-one credit report with data from Equifax, Experian and TransUnion, along with credit scores; daily alerts by e-mail, phone and text messaging notifying one of personal information changes, credit inquiries, changes to existing accounts and any new accounts or public records added; free credit analysis and identity-theft insurance up to $20,000.

TRUCREDIT

$24.95/month for the first month, $14.95/month thereafter; unlimited access to credit reports and scores

A three-in-one credit report with data from Equifax, Experian and TransUnion, along with credit scores; daily alerts within twenty-four hours by e-mail, phone and text messaging notifying one of personal information changes, credit inquiries, changes to existing accounts and any new accounts or public records added; free credit analysis and identity-theft insurance up to $25,000.

Source: Compiled from the companies' Web sites

credit-reporting agencies, but if you decide to do this, be sure to print the claim for your records.

By law, the agencies have just thirty days to respond to your request to fix the error, and they must notify other agencies of the correction if the error has dented your score. If you don't like the response you get from the credit-reporting agency, you can mail the agency a letter explaining your side of the story and ask that it be permanently attached to your file. For more egregious errors, you may want to consult an attorney.

You should regularly review your credit report, keeping an eagle eye out for such things as unrecognizable names, a change of address, accounts you don't recall opening or past-due notices on accounts that you did open in the past but no longer use. You are allowed one free credit report annually from each bureau. You can order a free annual report from each of the three major credit-reporting bureaus online at annualcreditreport.com, or by calling (877) 322-8228. If you stagger your requests for free reports throughout the year, you'll be reviewing one of your reports every four months.

If you don't have the time or the inclination to monitor your credit reports this diligently, many companies, including the credit-reporting agencies themselves, are offering credit-report monitoring services—for a price. Costs for services that may include access to your credit score (the number lenders use to determine your creditworthiness), identity-theft insurance and daily e-mail alerts range from around $6.66 to $14.95 a month.

It pays to detect a stolen identity yourself rather than find out from a third party. Cases of identity theft that were detected by the victim resulted in consumer costs that averaged $347, while cases that were discovered by others resulted in costs averaging $538, according to a 2006 survey by Javelin Strategy & Research and the Better Business Bureau.

Using your credit report to prevent identity theft is even better than using it to detect theft, but doing so is not always easy. Several states allow consumers to issue a "freeze" on their credit reports, meaning that the credit bureau cannot release your credit report to anyone without your explicit approval. Very few lenders are willing to extend credit without seeing a copy of an applicant's credit report, so the freeze stops an identity thief from using your information to obtain a loan. If you live in a state that requires a credit bureau to honor your request for a freeze, you still have to initiate the freeze with each credit bureau independently. Like a fraud alert, a freeze can be a stumbling block for consumers who need to apply for a new credit card or cell phone plan, but I think it's worth the extra hassle for the peace of mind it provides. Be aware, too, that your right to invoke this powerful protective weapon against fraud is in jeopardy, the result of a lobbying campaign by the powerful banking and credit-card industries. You may recall the bill I mentioned in Chapter 1 that if passed would deny you the right to place a freeze on your credit report unless you've already been the victim of fraud! That's already the situation in those states that have, for whatever reason, been unwilling to protect their citizens.

Is there a downside to freezing your credit report? You bet. First, it's probably going to cost you unless you've already been a victim of identity fraud. Florida, for instance, allows a credit bureau to assess a $10 fee to place, temporarily lift or permanently remove a credit freeze. And you'll be incurring that fee each time you want to apply for new credit. It also takes a few days to get the freeze temporarily lifted, so no more impulse purchases using a retailer's offer of discounts in exchange for signing up for the store's revolving charge card. And there's the inconvenience of keeping track of the PIN the credit bureau issues you when you first place the freeze. You'll need that PIN each time you want to lift the freeze.

CREDIT REPORTS AND CREDIT SCORES

I mentioned earlier that your credit report is the source of your credit score, which is compiled by Fair Isaac and by the three credit bureaus. While the score has nothing to do with identity

REPORT CARD

What's in a credit score? Here are the five categories of information that are typically used in calculating a credit score:

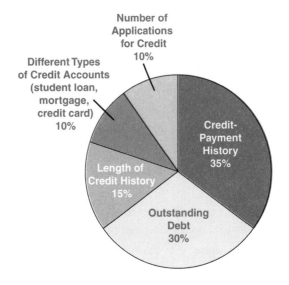

theft (unless yours is so bad that nobody will lend to you—and if that's the case you've got a whole different problem), it's worth knowing how the credit score is compiled and what it means for you. Fair Isaac and the three credit bureaus take information from your credit reports and plug it into complicated formulas that come up with a value representing the amount of risk you pose to a lender. That value takes into account the track record of other consumers with similar credit profiles. By looking at this value, or score, lenders are able to gauge roughly whether it's a good idea to extend you credit.

The FICO scale ranges from 300 to 850. To compensate for the risk that a borrower may welsh on new debt just as he or she did in the past, the lender increases the interest rate it charges him or her. So, the lower your score, the more you ultimately pay. The median score in the United States was 723 in mid-2005, with most (28 percent) in the 750 to 799 range.

KEEPING SCORE

How much can a low credit score cost you? Let's say you're home shopping and you'd like to borrow $200,000 on a thirty-year, fixed-rate mortgage. According to the loan-savings calculator on MyFico.com (www.myfico.com), your monthly payment can differ as much as $460 a month depending on your credit score. Here are different rates lenders might have charged in mid-2005, based on different credit scores, and how the rates affect monthly mortgage payments:

FICO Score	% APR	Monthly Payment	Total Interest Paid
720–850	5.937%	$1,191	$228,764
700–719	6.062	$1,207	$234,551
675–699	6.599	$1,277	$259,787
620–674	7.749	$1,433	$315,767
560–619	8.531	$1,542	$355,200
500–559	9.289	$1,651	$394,362

Source: Copyright © Fair Isaac Corporation. Used with permission.

Mismanaging your credit has a very real impact. In this example, assuming the homeowner remained in the home through the entire thirty-year term, someone with bad credit would pay nearly $165,600 more in interest than a good borrower with a top credit score.

The FICO score isn't the only score out there. The big three credit-reporting agencies—which each marketed their own in-house scoring system—in 2006 introduced a new score based on their combined scores. It is called the Vantage score, and its purpose is to compete with FICO. There is no single, industry-wide definition of good credit because different lenders look differently upon different scores—and even that can change from one day to the next, depending upon the type of business a particular lender is looking to attract at some given point. In general, however, you never want a credit score to drop below the 700 range, where consumers are charged substantially higher on so-called sub-prime loans. Ideally, a score in the mid-700s will qualify you for the best deals around.

Different scores can be required for different types of loan applications. For example, because a mortgage represents a significant amount of credit over a long repayment period, creditors will usually require a high score to qualify for the best deals. The purchase of a cell phone plan obviously does not require such a high score.

CASE STUDY

A CLOSER LOOK AT AN EXCELLENT, A BAD AND AN AVERAGE CREDIT REPORT

Personal-finance writers are constantly urging readers to check their credit reports regularly, both to fix any errors that may dent their credit score and to stay on guard for signs of identity theft.

Credit-reporting companies compile data on how many credit-card accounts, loans and mortgages you've opened and closed throughout your life—along with any public court documents detailing any bankruptcies, liens or foreclosures against you. Credit-scoring companies take this information and use proprietary formulas to come up with your credit score.

In fact, that's one reason there's so much confusion about credit scores—there's no single formula used for calculating them. Fair Isaac is the creator of the FICO credit score that many mortgage companies use. And credit-reporting companies such as Equifax, Experian and TransUnion each use their own scoring formulas. Then, in 2006, the three credit-reporting agencies announced plans to introduce a joint scoring method called a Vantage score. Each weigh some factors differently, but generally all agree that there are certain behaviors that separate the responsible borrowers from the reckless ones.

In this section, I'll walk you through one sample credit report of a hypothetical consumer with an excellent credit score, one with a low credit score and one with an average credit score. Fortunately, some credit-reporting companies are doing a much better job at making credit reports easier to read, so it's easier for consumers to identify negative information and errors that may be harming their credit score.

FICO FORMULA

These are some of the components that make up your FICO score.

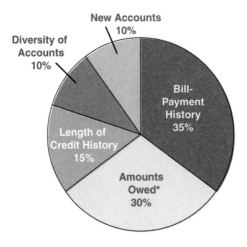

*Especially balance-to-limit ratios

AN EXCELLENT CREDIT SCORE

Let's start at the top with the credit score of Hugo N. Nightingale, a hypothetical individual with an excellent credit score. Generally, if your score is 750 or above, you'll qualify for the best deals lenders are offering. Hugo's FICO score is 783 out of a possible 850. Nearly 80 percent of all U.S. consumers have credit scores that are lower than Hugo's score.

According to FICO, a score in this range makes it extremely unlikely that Hugo's application for a credit card or a mortgage would be turned down. Consumers with scores between 750 and 799 have an account delinquency rate of 2 percent according to Fair Isaac, meaning just two borrowers out of one hundred are likely to miss payments on their credit-card accounts or default on a loan. (In comparison, borrowers with credit scores in the 550 to 599 range have a delinquency rate of 51 percent.)

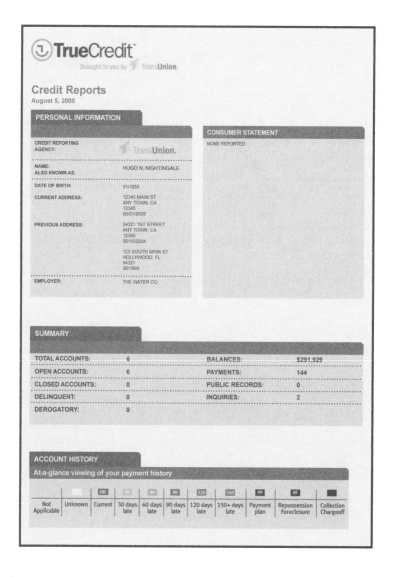

Hugo's relatively high score means he'll likely qualify for higher-than-average credit limits, the lowest rates and other rewards or incentives the lenders may offer. Several factors boosted Hugo's score. First, he has never made a late payment on any of his credit accounts. (He's not alone: More than 68 percent of Americans haven't missed a single credit payment in the past, says Fair Isaac.) Borrowers who've made late payments in the past are likelier to make late payments in the

[95]

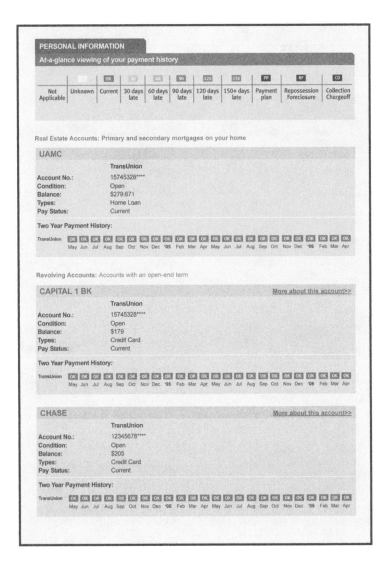

future. This is why late payments weigh so heavily on your credit score. The scoring formula will look at how many late payments you've made in the past across all of your accounts. The score also factors in whether the payments were thirty, sixty or ninety-plus days past due—obviously payments that are sixty days or more past due weigh more heavily on your score than those a month or less late. The score also takes into account how recently you've made late payments: A bunch of

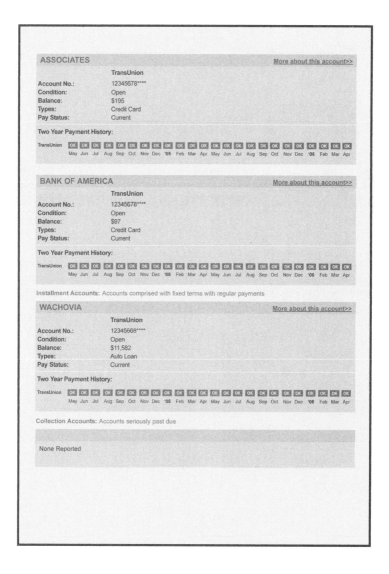

late payments made ten years ago will harm your score less than one or two made in the last six months.

In addition to paying his bills on time, Hugo has another positive factor affecting his credit score—he isn't maxing out his revolving credit lines (credit-card accounts such as Visa, Mastercard, American Express, Discover and department-store credit cards). Generally, lenders like to see no more than 50 percent of the total credit line used at any given time. This

PUBLIC INFORMATION

At-a-glance viewing of your payment history

None Reported

INQUIRIES

Creditor Name	Date of Inquiry	Credit Bureau
UAMC	12/29/2004	TransUnion
WACHOVIA	01/02/2005	TransUnion

CREDITOR CONTACTS

Creditor Name	Address	Phone Number
UAMC	POB 21906 DAYTON, OH 45501	888-555-1234
ASSOCIATES	POB 96521 PLAINFIELD, NJ, 08061	888-555-5678
BANK OF AMERICA	664 TORO ST SAN LUIS OBISPO, CA 93501	888-555-9101
CAPITAL ONE BANK	155 N LAKE AVE MS 3 162 PASADENA , CA 91201	888-555-1213
CHASE BANK	POB 77279 HOUSTON , TX 78279	888-555-1415
WACHOVIA BANK	POB 30529 WILMINGTON, DE 19701	888-555-1617

is often called a "balance-to-limit" ratio. (Many credit-card holders who consolidate all of their outstanding balances onto one low-interest-rate card often unwittingly damage their scores as a result.)

Hugo's balance-to-limit ratio is just 2 percent, compared to the average carried by consumers of around 34 percent, according to Fair Isaac. People with higher-than-average balances on their credit lines are deemed riskier than people with lower

RANKING THE RISK

This chart shows the delinquency rate of individuals with certain credit scores. The delinquency rate is the percentage of borrowers with accounts ninety or more days past due or those with other more serious situations such as bankruptcy or foreclosure. (These are FICO scores only; other credit-reporting companies use their own scoring, which may not match these scores.)

FICO Score	Delinquency Risk
Up to 499	83%
500–549	70%
550–599	51%
600–649	31%
650–699	14%
700–749	5%
750–799	2%
800+	1%

Source: Copyright © Fair Isaac Corporation. Used with permission.

outstanding balances. High balances may count against you even if you pay your credit card off in full each month, since some companies report the outstanding balance at the last billing statement.

Hugo's relatively long credit history also proves he's an experienced borrower. His credit history goes back more than ten years. On average, Fair Isaac says, consumers have a credit history of fourteen to fifteen years. Why does the length of your history matter? Lenders can get a much more accurate picture of your borrowing behavior over time than they can if you've been using credit for only a few years.

Hugo also has experience borrowing with different types

of credit accounts. In addition to revolving credit-card accounts, he has opened installment accounts, such as those used to pay for student loans or mortgages. Lenders like to see borrowers who can successfully manage a variety of accounts.

Finally, Hugo has no history of dealing with collection agencies and no public records on file that would be perceived as being a negative—information such as court judgments, tax liens, garnishments, bankruptcies or foreclosures.

Although Hugo's personal information isn't used to determine his FICO score, some lenders frown on people like Hugo who have numerous former addresses or employers or people who have taken out credit under aliases. Lenders ultimately are looking for stability, both in the way you manage your life and your credit.

Still, Hugo's score isn't in the 800s for a reason. The one negative factor keeping his score down is the fact that he opened a new credit line relatively recently. His last new account was opened seventeen months ago; the average consumer opened his or her most recent new account twenty months ago. Lenders have found that individuals who open new credit lines frequently are more likely to miss payments. The good news is that Hugo's score will continue to improve as the months pass without him opening any new credit lines.

A BAD CREDIT SCORE

Now that we've seen what an excellent credit report looks like, let's take a look at the credit report of an individual with a low score. Meet Gertrude Harkernreader: Poor Gertrude has a FICO score of 574, well below the average score of around 725. All lenders have differing tolerances for risk, so there's no "cut-off score" that would prevent Gertrude from obtaining some form of credit. Still, because her score is so low, the types of credit offers she might receive from so-called sub-prime lenders would be limited, and those lenders that do extend her credit will likely charge her the highest rates for low-

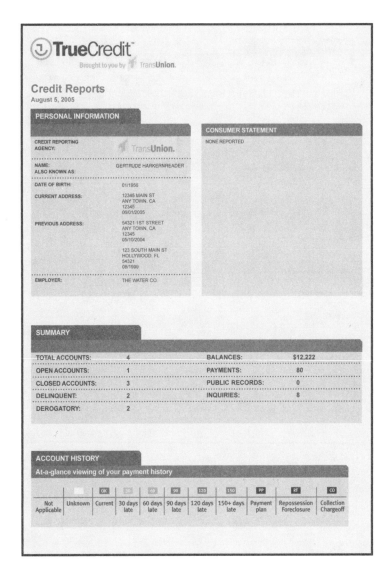

balance credit lines. Depending on the loan, some lenders may require some form of collateral or a cosigner.

Several factors hurt Gertrude's score. Her late-payment history is first among them. Gertrude has accounts with delinquent payments that are sixty days past due or greater. Roughly 27 percent of U.S. consumers have this type of negative information on their credit reports. As I noted before, studies show that if you've made late payments in the past, you're far more

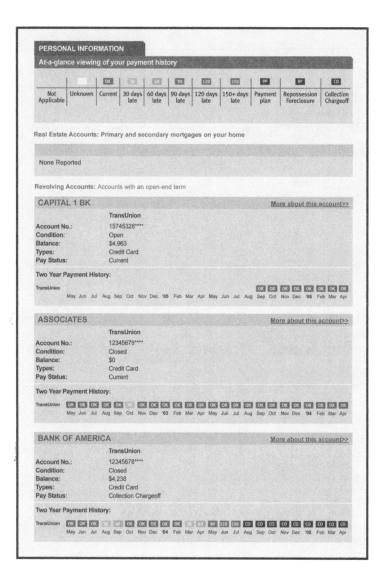

likely to pay your bills late in the future. Particularly damning is that Gertrude incurred her late payments recently, one just three months ago. About 46 percent of consumers have at least one late payment on their reports, but on average the delinquency occurred nineteen months before the date of the credit report. Recent late payments count more heavily against your credit score than late payments recorded years ago. It's a sign

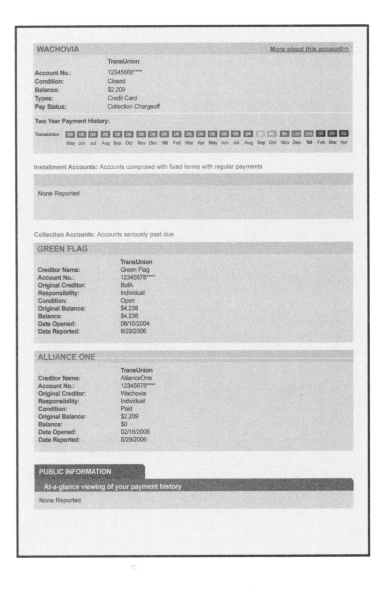

to lenders that you may currently be in financial distress. That said, one random late payment on an account may not count as heavily against you if you've continued to make all of your payments in a timely fashion since then.

Gertrude has also been delinquent on more than one account. There are four accounts to which she's made late payments. The average for consumers with delinquencies in their

INQUIRIES

Creditor Name	Date of Inquiry	Credit Bureau
INFRM RESRCH	12/05/2004	TransUnion
UAMC	12/29/2004	TransUnion
WACHOVIA	01/02/2005	TransUnion
ASSOCIATES	06/15/2005	TransUnion
BANK OF AMERICA	08/28/2005	TransUnion
CAPITAL ONE BANK	02/11/2006	TransUnion
CHASE BANK	04/21/2006	TransUnion
FDC	07/21/2006	TransUnion

CREDITOR CONTACTS

Creditor Name	Address	Phone Number
ASSOCIATES	POB 96521 PLAINFIELD, NJ, 08061	888-555-5678
BANK OF AMERICA	664 TORO ST SAN LUIS OBISPO, CA 93501	888-555-9101
CAPITAL ONE BANK	155 N LAKE AVE MS 3 162 PASADENA , CA 91201	888-555-1213
WACHOVIA BANK	POB 30529 WILMINGTON, DE 19701	888-555-1617
INFRM RESRCH	POB 21562 WHITE PLAINS, NY 19701	888-555-1819
UAMC	225 N MAIN AVE MS 2 153 MONROVIA , CA 91501	888-555-2021
CHASE BANK	POB 54321 HOUSTON , TX 77279	888-555-2223
FDC	POB 68951 PLANO , TX 78209	888-555-2425
GREEN FLAG	POB 98765 DAYTON, OH 54321	888-555-2627
ALLIANCE ONE	POB 25498 ELIZABETH, NJ 11543	888-555-2829

files is two. Multiple delinquencies, particularly if the payments were missed recently, are a very powerful negative.

With all of these late payments made on several accounts, just about the only thing Gertrude can do to improve her score is to find a way to stay current on her monthly bills. Most crucially, she should make mortgage payments in full and on time, since lenders view late mortgage payments more seriously than late payments on other types of credit. If she can do so, in time her credit score will rise.

Next, Gertrude's balance-to-limit ratio is a sky-high 118 percent; compare that to the average consumer who has a ratio of just 34 percent. Gertrude is in over her head. Although it's not a good option for Gertrude, one way to reduce that ratio would be to open another credit-card account and shift some of the balance to another card. Such a tactic would not work for Gertrude because it's likely that any credit line she manages to obtain will come with loan-shark-like rates. And any card or loan she might obtain would be viewed as an account opened recently, another negative that would hurt her score.

A better option for Gertrude is to pay her bills more strategically to lower the ratio over time: Gertrude should make the minimum monthly payments due on revolving credit-card accounts that have the lowest balances with the lowest interest rates and funnel as much additional cash as she can toward paying down accounts with high balances and high finance charges. So, for example, Gertrude has a department-store card that's near maxed-out and charging a 39 percent penalty rate because she's missed some payments. She also has another revolving store card with only a few hundred dollars outstanding at a relatively low 21 percent rate. Gertrude should pay the minimum on the revolving store card and focus on bringing down the balance on that maxed-out card first.

Another good reason for Gertrude to avoid opening any more new accounts is the number of "inquiries" already on her report. When companies such as lenders want to make offers of pre-approved credit, they make so-called soft inquiries on your credit report to gauge your creditworthiness. (When you check your own credit report, it's also considered a soft inquiry.) Soft inquiries aren't used to determine your credit score. However, if you give someone such as a lender or potential employer or landlord permission to check your report, it shows up as a "hard inquiry" that *is* factored into your score.

Every time a hard inquiry is made, it appears on your

credit report, and the more inquiries that are made the worse your credit score will be. This is because multiple applications for credit in a short period of time indicates that the borrower is in financial distress. (One or two inquiries usually have an insignificant impact on your score.) Gertrude has seven. Credit-scoring firms typically look back only to hard inquiries that have happened in the past twelve months, so if Gertrude refrains from trying to open a new credit account, her score will begin to improve.

There aren't many factors in Gertrude's favor. Her borrowing history is long at twenty-four years, which lenders like to see. If she has very old accounts that are still open, but not being used, she should leave them open. If she closes them, it would effectively shorten her credit history and knock down her score. That said, old dormant accounts are ripe targets for identity thieves, since account holders aren't paying attention to them. For that reason, always be sure to check your credit report regularly for any signs of recent activity.

If you've made some serious mistakes with credit in the past and your credit report looks something like this one, don't panic. While your current credit score is based on your borrowing history, it's your future borrowing behavior that will help improve your score. Negative information remains on your credit report for up to seven years, when reporting firms are required to delete it. (More serious infractions, such as judgments and foreclosures, remain for up to ten years.) Going forward, work at proving you've become a more responsible borrower by paying your bills on time and your credit score will steadily increase as those negative accounts disappear from your record.

AN AVERAGE CREDIT SCORE

Hugo and Gertrude are at the extremes of credit scoring. Now let's look at John Q. Public, whose average FICO score of 720 falls right near the national median of 723. Lenders of all

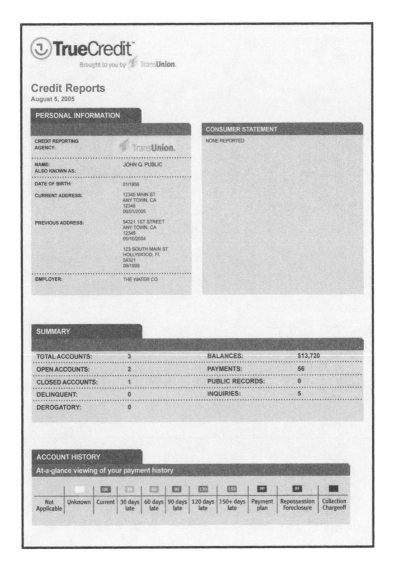

stripes are usually eager to do business with him, though he may not qualify for the very best deals. Unlike Gertrude, who needs to clean up after the mess she's made of her credit history, John needs to be careful not to screw up in the future. John has a relatively long history of various types of credit accounts, with perhaps a missed payment or two showing up many years ago when he was younger and less well-off financially. Though it dents your credit score, lenders usually are willing

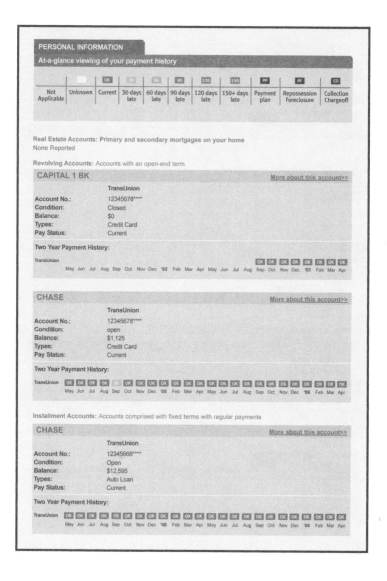

to overlook these past mistakes as long as the borrower has made timely payments in the years since then. As with Hugo and Gertrude, if John stays on top of his monthly bills and makes future payments on time and older negative entries gradually fall off his reports, his credit score should gradually improve.

At $8,200, John has slightly less than the average $9,000 in credit-card debt that a typical borrower has at any given time,

Collection Accounts: Accounts seriously past due

None Reported

PUBLIC INFORMATION

At-a-glance viewing of your payment history

None Reported

INQUIRIES

Creditor Name	Date of Inquiry	Credit Bureau
INFRM RESRCH	12/29/2004	TransUnion
CENTRAL INDUSTRIAL FINANCIAL	01/02/2005	TransUnion
UNIVERSAL CREDIT	11/01/2005	TransUnion
LANDSAFE CREDIT	01/12/2006	TransUnion
FDC	04/08/2006	TransUnion

CREDITOR CONTACTS

Creditor Name	Address	Phone Number
CENTRAL INDUSTRIAL FINANCIAL	664 TORO ST SAN LUIS OBISPO, CA 93401	888-555-1234
NAUTILUS FINANCIAL	664 TORO ST SAN LUIS OBISPO, CA 93401	888-555-5678
UNIVERSAL CREDIT	664 TORO ST SAN LUIS OBISPO, CA 93401	888-555-9101
CAPITAL ONE BANK	155 N LAKE AVE MS 3 162 PASADENA , CA 91101	888-555-1213
CHASE BANK	POB 77279 HOUSTON , TX 77279	888-555-1415

and it's spread out across a variety of accounts, which lenders like to see. He does have one department-store card that's close to being maxed-out—not because he's a shopaholic but because it has a very low credit limit, pushing his balance-to-limit ratio higher. John should pay off the card immediately and avoid using it in the future. He should also check to ensure that any past accounts he closed are reflected on the report as being "closed at the customer's request." Accounts that are marked as being closed by the lenders are seen as negatives that may hurt your score, particularly if they are accounts for which the lender reported delinquent payments.

The five hard inquiries showing up on John's report can also dent his credit score. Perhaps John's been credit-card hopping to find the latest 0-percent financing deals or perhaps he switched cell phone plans yet again. John needs to keep in mind that every hard inquiry is another knock to his score and borrow more carefully, particularly if it's likely he'll need to apply for a mortgage in the near future. (The good news is that lenders don't generally hold multiple inquiries against you when it's clear you're comparison shopping for a mortgage or an auto loan.) Finally, John's got a nice stable job, a reassuring sign of stability.

CHAPTER 5

THE TECH WARS

Dumpster diving, with its pronounced "yuck!" factor, is probably the lowest form of identity theft. At the other end of the spectrum is technology, which allows thieves to sneak into your life and steal your identity via electrons. It's a sophisticated world and getting more so every day. If you or someone in your family uses a computer to go online at home, work or school, you're a potential victim.

This is an area none of us can ignore, but it isn't always easy to understand. In this chapter, I'll attempt to steer the middle ground between tech talk that only the geeks will understand and getting so simplistic that the average computer user won't learn anything useful. We'll look at two major ways that scamsters use technology to steal your identity. The first way makes you an accomplice to the theft since you willingly—albeit innocently—provide the thieves with all the information they could possibly want. The second way is done without your knowledge, as phantom programs are loaded onto your computer that send information about you back to the thieves. Hundreds of thousands of computers are infected with these programs, referred to by such descriptive nicknames as "Trojans" (remember the horse?) and "bots," geek slang for robots.

The tech wars over identity theft have escalated rapidly in the last decade. In the early 1990s, hackers were generally teens

DATA WOES

Companies reporting types of incidents, among more than 500 companies surveyed

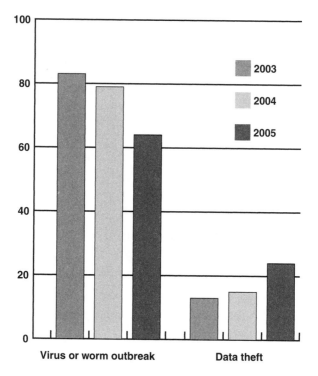

Source: Yankee Group

or computer enthusiasts looking to build a reputation in their online community by devising and sending out computer viruses and worms. One of the most notorious, the "I Love You" virus, spawned in 2000, spread to an estimated 45 million e-mail accounts in a single day. Security experts say many hackers are no longer in it for fun. Today, they're much more aware of the wealth of information that can be harvested online for profit or malicious intent. One of the new buzzwords in the Internet security business is "malware," short for malicious software.

Individual computer owners are having a hard enough time trying to combat viruses, worms and spam—and more recently spyware, adware and phishing schemes—that seek to obtain sensitive information. But the corporate security experts are engaged in a day-by-day struggle of epic proportions as they fend off nearly constant attacks and probes of their networks by criminals or disgruntled employees attempting to steal consumer information.

Indeed, the first half of the decade has seen a marked increase in attacks by hackers against some of the largest financial institutions in the world. Security experts say it's likely these types of attacks will become more brazen as technology evolves. Increasingly complex technologies continually introduce weaknesses into companies' computer systems that smart predators can exploit. In 2005, the computer-protection software maker Symantec issued a report that noted a significant decrease in the number of large-scale global virus outbreaks and a simultaneous increase in smaller, more focused attacks.

The consequences of this trend are ominous. In 2005, the Department of Homeland Security prepared a worst-case cyber-disaster scenario in which crooks broke into financial-services facilities and wreaked havoc on the entire system. In that nightmare scenario, automated teller machines failed nationwide, some 20 million credit cards were canceled and computer malfunctions caused a week-long shutdown of pension and mutual-fund companies. The department's conclusion? Americans would lose faith in the entire U.S. financial system.

But it's not all gloom and doom. Just as software programs were designed to combat garden-variety computer cranks, security experts are coming up with new ways to keep consumers and businesses safe from emerging online threats, and we'll examine some of their offerings later in the chapter. For all the sophisticated technologies, however, you're still the first line of defense against scamsters. That's especially true when fraudsters go on "phishing" expeditions and invite you to join them.

PHISHING FRAUD

The origin of the term "phishing" isn't entirely clear, but there's general agreement that it applies the common hacker replacement of the letter "f" with "ph" and refers to the methodology of using a "lure"—a Web site or an e-mail—to fish for passwords and personal information. The term first emerged in the mid-1990s when hackers were stealing America Online accounts by scamming passwords from AOL users. Today, phishing encompasses a much broader range of targets, including online banking and retailing, and is growing quickly in both sophistication and frequency of occurrence.

A typical phishing scheme looks deceptively simple. Let's say you do online banking through Citibank. One day, you get an e-mail that certainly appears to have come from Citibank. It includes the company's logo, and the return e-mail address features a term like "UserSupport9@Citibank.com," which looks realistic enough. The e-mail informs you that Citibank's technical services group has been updating its software and that you should follow the Web link contained in the message to confirm your data. If you don't confirm your data, the e-mail warns, "your access to the system may be blocked."

Hmm, you sure don't want your access blocked, so you click on the link—something like https://web.data-us.citibank.com/signin/scripts/login2/user.setup.jsp—and are promptly sent to another Web site that still looks like an official Citibank Web site. This Web site includes a familiar-looking screen with boxes for all kinds of information, including your Social Security number, your checking-account and debit-card numbers, your Citibank user ID and password, the PIN for your ATM access and the numbers for your Citibank credit cards, including the expiration date. It even includes that most familiar of all security devices—a box for your mother's maiden name. Fill out the data boxes, press "submit" and you're once again able to gain access to your Citibank online accounts. Trouble is, you never lost that access. Neither the e-mail nor the Web site to which you were directed to provide all that vital information has anything to do with the real Citibank. It's all forged, and that "submit" button sent all your data straight to a criminal's computer, where it will either be used to rob you directly or sold on the Internet so that someone else can rob you.

Of course *you* wouldn't have been fooled, would you? But the sad truth is that hundreds are fooled every day. A typical phishing scheme involves sending thousands of similar e-mails. Most people don't respond. But it takes only a few responses to provide the phishermen with a lucrative haul of information.

While the example I've used looks simple enough to execute, it really isn't easy to conduct a massive, well-constructed phishing scheme. True, you can learn to do it on the Internet—some experts estimate it would probably take a day or so and you would have to spend about $30 to set up a fake Web site—but chances are you'd make a mistake or two that would sharply limit your response rate from victims. It takes an unusual combination of psychological insight and computer skills to put together a fake Web site and a message to elicit the maximum number of responses from victims. To send out a sufficient number of e-mails to get a reasonable number of responses, the phisher has to scan huge numbers of Internet addresses to find an unsecured "host" computer or server that can then be used to issue the e-mails. Often the phishing thief joins forces with spammers, who have databases containing millions of active e-mail addresses. Spam is often sent from servers in other countries, so tracking down the origin of spam or of a phishing scheme is difficult.

The best defense against falling victim to a phishing scheme is simply to not bite when the lure is dangled before you. Legitimate financial concerns *do not* ask for detailed financial information over the Internet. Therefore, you should never send that information over the Internet.

As I noted in Chapter 3, there are a number of ways to verify that a Web site is legitimate and secure. Before making a transaction, first check to make sure it's a secure site by looking for a Web address that starts with "https://" instead of "http://." The VeriSign Secured™ Seal is another indicator (though it is possible that a phishing scheme can copy the seal). Next look for the lock icon at the lower-right corner of your browser window. An open or broken lock is a sign that your information may not be protected by encryption. If you're still unsure, check to make sure a company is a legitimate business on sites such as the Better Business Bureau (www.bbbonline.org) and TRUSTe (www.truste.com). Or call the business yourself—a Web site with no telephone contact information is a red flag signaling possible risk.

ATTACK OF THE TROJANS

A phishing scheme that induces your cooperation is fairly easy to avoid: Just say NO! But there are other threats out there that don't require your help, and they're particularly insidious, burying themselves deep in your computer, where they operate to do their evil silently. That's why security experts are more concerned about these newer types of invasive programs that are harder to catch and potentially more dangerous.

Typically, these invasions involve a software program called a "Trojan," named, obviously, after the legendary wooden

Greek horse that led to the downfall of Troy. Computer users unwittingly download programs from Web sites that appear to be perfectly harmless, but buried within the code is a Trojan "key logger" program designed to record their keystrokes and automatically transmit the information back to a criminal—all without the users' knowledge. Other Trojan programs search out file names that include the word "password" or "account" and transmit that information. Still others routinely capture screen shots of your Web surfing and broadcast the slideshow to criminals, who can use the information for purposes of account-information theft or even blackmail.

How devious can these programs be? One audacious Trojan, Cryzip, discovered in early 2006, automatically encrypted certain commonly used files, such as documents or pictures, on a victim's PC and then demanded that a ransom of $300 be paid before the victim received a password to access the encrypted files. The program provided step-by-step instructions on where to send the ransom money and how to access the files!

A good way to avoid attracting Trojans is to keep your computer protected with up-to-date security patches and antivirus software, though these programs aren't infallible. Many Trojan programs are customized to attack a specific target—say to transmit keystrokes that are made only on a particular Web site. These types of threats may not pop up on a virus scanner's radar because the software is designed to spot and block only previously identified computer threats. It's also a good idea to avoid opening e-mail attachments—even from someone you know. That cute photo your sister passed along to everyone on her buddy list may contain something sinister. Also avoid downloading programs whenever possible, particularly from unfamiliar Web sites.

BEWARE THE "BOTS"

The most-recent form of computer hijacking involves bots— short for "robots." Bots enter your computer as a Trojan, but instead of monitoring your computer files and activity, these programs essentially allow a hacker to take over your computer. Bots target thousands of vulnerable PCs and create a network that criminals can use to send out spam or phishing e-mails to others in an attempt to steal bank-account numbers and other personal information. To some victims, it may appear that the phishing e-mail is coming from you.

Increasingly aware of the danger, law enforcement is cracking down. In November 2005, a federal grand jury in California indicted a twenty-year-old Downey, California, man with conspiracy to cause damage to a computer, accessing a computer to conduct fraud and money laundering and other charges. The man earned thousands of dollars by hijacking computers and then renting out access to networks of as many as ten thousand machines to people who wanted to launch Internet attacks and send spam. A month earlier, Dutch police arrested three men who had created a bot network of 1.5 million computers, which it used to steal identities and distribute spyware.

Unfortunately, home PCs are at risk of becoming victims of bots because software makers have yet to offer sophisticated network-monitoring tools that would flag them. If you suddenly notice that your inbox is receiving a bunch of e-mails you never sent, all being kicked back to you as undeliverable, chances are your computer may be infected. Microsoft and other software vendors have programs, some of which are free, that can be purchased or downloaded that seek out and destroy bots. It's well worth the effort to install a bot-detecting program on each of your computers.

HIJACKING YOUR PDA

Most people are aware of the dangers hackers pose to their home computers, but few realize how vulnerable their other electronic devices may be to cyber-criminals. Many personal digital assistants (PDAs) and so-called smart phones, which allow you to access the Internet and company computer networks, have wireless connections that are always on. This makes the devices more susceptible to viruses, worms and the theft of personal information.

Mobile viruses are spread by downloading Internet content, receiving text messages and using Bluetooth, a form of short-range wireless communication. The problem is expected to grow as more users adopt smart-phone technology. In 2004, these devices accounted for just 3 percent of all handsets sold, but are expected to make up 27 percent of the total by 2009, according to research firm Gartner Inc. And wireless networks are becoming faster, allowing users to download more applications to their devices and expanding the number of Web sites users might access that may contain viruses.

If you use a device with a wireless connection that's always on, take advantage of security features that block unauthorized users from communicating with the device. Also be sure to change your password frequently. And don't let your wireless carrier off the hook—ask a sales representative or your carrier's customer-service agent what types of protection the company provides and what the company suggests you should do to make your device more secure.

KIDS CAN COMPROMISE YOUR COMPUTER

You may think hackers breaking into your computer is the biggest online threat, but you'd be wrong. The biggest problem is having your kids invite them in.

Web sites that offer "cheat" codes to enhance play on video games, video- and music-sharing services, social-interaction and, unfortunately, pornography are sometimes used by thieves to trick children into downloading software that can put your personal information at risk.

When my fifteen-year-old nephew came to visit last year and asked if he could use my computer to check his e-mail, I said sure—not realizing a criminal onslaught was about to

ROGUES GALLERY

Who's out there trying to tap into your PC? Here are some of the main players in cyber-theft:

HACKERS

Hackers break into networks for the thrill of the challenge or for bragging rights in the hacker community.

PHISHERS

Phishers are individuals or small groups who use fraudulent e-mail and Web sites to extract personal information from their victims that can then be used for monetary gain.

SPYWARE/MALWARE AUTHORS

These individuals or organizations have a malicious intent and carry out attacks against users by producing and distributing malware, like viruses or worms, and spyware, which is software secretly put on victims' computers to gather information about them.

ORGANIZED CRIME GROUPS

Criminal groups use spam, phishing and malware to commit identity theft and online fraud.

Source: The Wall Street Journal.

barrage my PC. A quick peek at the computer screen showed my virus-scanning software was at Defcon 1, alerting me repeatedly to the appearance of multiple viruses, spyware and other types of intrusive programs attacking my computer from a seemingly harmless video-game site he was visiting. I promptly booted him off the computer and rushed to make sure I had downloaded the latest version of my firewall and virus-scanning software. Luckily, no apparent damage was done.

Ideally, you should aggressively monitor your kids' online activity and use parental control and Internet-filtering software to keep them from going to suspicious or inappropriate Web sites. Some parents may want to consider software programs that allow them to monitor what their kids are doing online in real-time. Also, urge your kids to use search engines such as Yahoo's Yahooligans or Ask Jeeves's Ask Jeeves Kids, which will steer kids clear of unsavory or questionable Web sites. And, just as you warn your kids about safety threats in the real world, make sure they're aware of the potential threats online.

Security experts say even this may not be enough to protect your PC; some recommend that parents get separate computers—one for mom and dad, another for the kids.

PROTECTING YOUR PC

If you access the Internet from your home computer, you have a one-in-three chance of suffering computer damage, financial loss or both at the hands of a computer virus or spyware, according to a 2005 survey of online consumers by *Consumer Reports* magazine.

Keeping hackers and scammers at bay typically requires multiple software programs—spam and spyware blockers, virus scanners and firewall and privacy protectors. Depending on the software you choose, most need to be purchased and installed separately and require individual passwords and time-consuming upgrades. None are capable of spotting and blocking every possible threat—mainly because criminals are so creative at inventing new ways to use your computer against you.

According to *The Wall Street Journal*'s technology expert Walt Mossberg, "It's as if you had in your house a completely separate burglar alarm for the upstairs windows and the back

LEAVING THE DOORS UNLOCKED

Rates of installation of security software in U.S. homes with one PC

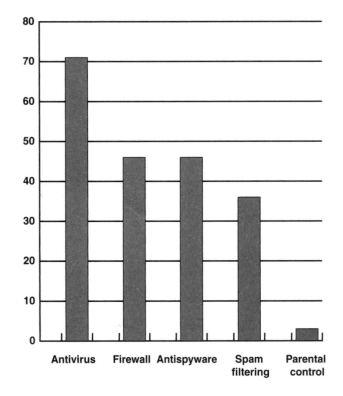

*Source: Copyright © 2000–2006 JupiterResearch, a division of JupiterKagan, Inc.,
survey of 2,275 online households in December 2005*

door and the downstairs windows. And when you walked in, there were four panels where you had to type in your passwords." Worse, users are forced to purchase and download newer versions of the software each year. It's enough to discourage people from using a PC at all.

Not surprisingly, many computer users avoid the problem altogether by doing nothing. Just 51 percent of U.S. PC users surveyed said they installed antispyware software, though 76 percent said they'd installed antivirus software, according to a 2006 survey by JupiterResearch. Microsoft has estimated that

roughly 70 percent of PC users either haven't installed antivirus protection software or did but failed to renew their
subscriptions.

Still, you want as much protection as possible to prevent a
thief from accessing your personal files. The bottom line is that
every computer should have antivirus and antispyware software along with a firewall (technology that acts as a barrier between your PC and the computer network). Here is a look at
some of your options:

SINGLE SOLUTION SOFTWARE

You'll spend more for tools that target individual dangers, but
in many cases, you'll find that companies that specialize in one
area of security provide a superior product. By picking the best
in show of security tools for each threat, you can build the
strongest security fence possible. Prices range anywhere from
free to $150 or more, depending on the vendors you choose.
You'll also need to factor in the time you'll need to spend eval-
uating the various tools in consumer magazines and Web sites.
(See the latest chart ranking single-solution antispam, antivirus and antispyware tools by *Consumer Reports*.)

One advantage to piecing your security tools together is
that you can make sure you're purchasing the best software
available in every category each year—so, if you decide to switch
vendors for, say, antispyware, you don't have to change all of
the software as you would with an all-in-one suite of tools.

ALL-IN-ONE SERVICES

Perhaps the easiest solution to protecting your PC is to choose
a company that bundles a bunch of protection programs all
into one service. Security-software makers such as McAfee,
Symantec and the Zone Labs unit of Check Point Software
Technologies offer services that include the three necessary security tools I mentioned for prices that range from about $50

BUILDING A BETTER SAFETY NET

By 2007, some major software makers are expected to roll out new services that aim to "automate" the way consumers protect and maintain their PCs—bundling a number of different computer-protection programs into one product that updates itself frequently. The programs will stop viruses, prevent "phishing" fraud, back up data and check up on a PC's overall health.

The new services are also altering the way users pay for keeping their antivirus protection up to date. Microsoft Corporation's upcoming Windows OneCare Live program will automatically monitor your PC's performance and fix problems when it finds them. It will also regularly upgrade software to combat new threats. Unlike typical antivirus software vendors, Microsoft plans to charge a flat annual fee for the service, and no new purchases or manual downloads will be necessary. Competing services, such as Symantec and McAfee, are expected to counter with their own service upgrades.

to $80 in mid-2006. These services can be bought off the shelf or downloaded from the software maker's Web site, though the programs expire after a year, and users must pay for and install new software each year after that.

There may be an additional cost involved if you need technical support. Symantec and McAfee typically charge users between $20 to $30 per call. A cheaper alternative is using Trend Micro's Internet Security suite, which offers free phone support.

One-stop shopping for Internet security tools makes sense for users who are confused by the array of programs out there. It also may be more cost-effective than buying software that targets individual problems. As I mentioned, companies that focus on combating one threat may provide a superior product to that of other companies with bundled services. For the latest rankings of the best antispam, antivirus and antispyware programs, you can check the *Consumer Reports* Web site at www.consumerreports.org.

FREEBIES

No-cost security tools have one obvious benefit—they're free. But you may pay dearly if you don't do your homework before installing the products. Like other freeware, many of these programs result in technical questions or problems. Don't expect much in the way of backup support to help you. Also, some of these programs require you to sign up for marketing lists prior to downloading the tools, which can lead to a ton of unwanted solicitations—in some cases, just the kind of spam you were trying to avoid in the first place!

Downloading and installing a free software program is also fraught with its own dangers: A number of free antispyware programs come embedded with spyware. The Web site SpywareWarrior.com lists a number of examples of this type of scam. Spend some time examining the Better Business Bureau's Web site at bbbonline.org and those of other online consumer-watchdog groups first to check for complaints about a vendor before downloading any free software from it.

THE LAPTOP: TECHNOLOGY'S WEAKEST LINK?

Once just a convenient tool for working outside of an office, some corporate laptop computers have become a veritable trove of valuable consumer information for identity thieves.

Over the last year alone, dozens of companies, organizations and government entities have reported that laptops containing identifiable information such as names, account numbers, birth dates and even Social Security numbers were lost or stolen. Remember from earlier chapters the most egregious incident: the theft in May 2006 of a laptop that contained the names, Social Security numbers and dates of birth of approximately 26.5 million veterans, military personnel and their spouses. The laptop was stolen during a burglary of a U.S. Department of Veterans Affairs employee's Maryland home. The employee wasn't authorized to take the data home, according to Veterans Affairs. The following month, the Federal Trade Commission said a laptop containing personal data had been stolen from one of its attorneys.

More troubling, most of the laptop thefts involved sensitive information that was password protected, but not encrypted. Encryption changes plain text to a secure code that requires a secret key or password to decrypt it.

In most cases, the motives for the thefts appear to be to steal and resell the stolen equipment rather than to access any information on the computers. And to date, no incidences of identity theft or fraud have ever been traced back to laptop thefts. Still, the numbers of consumers affected by lost or stolen data is staggering: More than 88 million Americans have been put at risk of identity theft from data security breaches since early 2005, according to the Privacy Rights Clearinghouse.

Data breaches cost companies an average of $5 million per incident in direct costs such as notifying victims, according to a study by the Ponemon Institute. The study also found that 20 percent of data-breach victims cut ties with institutions that have compromised their privacy.

Companies like Boeing and Aetna have begun to crack down on employees' use and management of laptops after both had laptops with sensitive data stolen from their employees. The moves come as many states introduce laws to encourage companies to do a better job at safeguarding consumer data. Several states, including California and Texas, allow individuals to sue organizations that fail to protect their sensitive information. Federal statutes also permit government agencies to sue organizations over data breaches.

LOOKING INTO
THE BREACH

The following companies, financial institutions and university are among the entities that reported that laptops containing sensitive personal information were stolen in 2006.

Company or organization	Type of business	No. of people effected	Type of data breached
Department of Veterans Affairs	Government agency	About 26.5 million	Names, dates of birth and Social Security numbers of veterans, military personnel and their spouses
Equifax	Credit-reporting company	2,500	Atlanta employee names and full and partial Social Security numbers
Federal Trade Commission	Government agency	110	Social Security numbers and other personal data on people involved in an ongoing legal case
Fidelity Investments	Financial services company	196,000	Sensitive personal information on current and former Hewlett-Packard employees
ING America	Financial services company	13,000	Retirement-account information on Washington, D.C., employees
University of California, Berkeley	Educational institution	100,000	Social Security numbers and other personal information on alumni, graduate students and applicants

Source: The Wall Street Journal. Online

Sadly, there's not much victims of laptop data breaches can do but monitor their credit reports and financial accounts for signs of suspicious activity. Workers who use laptops that may contain sensitive information—either theirs or someone else's—should consider whether that data is adequately protected. Have your company's technical support team install encryption and password-protection software (if it already hasn't done so). You can also purchase your own encryption software from vendors like Microsoft's Encryption File System, PGP's Whole Disk and Pointsec Mobile Technologies' Pointsec for PC.

PART II

LIFE AFTER
IDENTITY
THEFT

CHAPTER 6

GETTING YOUR IDENTITY BACK

Despite your best efforts, it's happened. You're a victim. Someone out there is using your personal information. What now?

Your first step is the same no matter what kind of identity theft or fraud is involved: Keep calm. Panicky responses in the form of telephone calls or e-mails to creditors or other financial institutions before you've collected your evidence and reviewed the proper procedures can make things worse. An initial claim that your identity is being used by someone else based on scanty information may mean that the record changes as you find out more details. Your changing story can then be used against you by creditors or others who become suspicious about the validity of your claims. Take a deep breath, consult this chapter (you should keep this book with your records so that you'll have a guide at hand to take you step by step through the procedure for discovering the crime and fixing its consequences) and then start a log with dates and times of the contacts you make with anyone about your problem. A sample format for such a log is in Appendix 2.

The FTC has a Web site for identity theft, with some helpful forms and other resources, at www.consumer.gov/idtheft.

Whom you contact and what you ask them to do will depend in large part on the nature of the identity theft. While every form of identity theft is disturbing, some are worse than others and demand more vigorous responses. Discovering that your Social Security number is being used by an imposter to obtain employment fraudulently is much less serious than finding out that someone is charging thousands of dollars of merchandise to your credit-card account—or, worse yet, that someone is removing money from your bank account. I'll start by outlining some standard procedures and contacts you can make for typical cases of identity theft, and then I'll get into the more vexing issues of dealing with collection agencies and other forms of harassment.

Social Security Fraud

In response to the example just mentioned—your Social Security card is being used by someone to obtain employment—you can go directly to the Social Security Administration's fraud hotline to file a complaint. To contact the administration online, go to www.socialsecurity.gov/oig. The toll-free number is (800) 269-0271. You should also send a written complaint to SSA Fraud Hotline, P.O. Box 17768, Baltimore, MD 21235. For state benefits, contact your state's Department of Labor. You can find a complete list of contact information on state labor departments online at www.dol.gov.

Don't ask immediately to change your Social Security number. A new Social Security number often causes more problems for a victim than it solves. With a new number, you essentially become a brand-new borrower with no credit history, thereby wrecking your credit score. Besides, the Social Security Administration won't issue a new number unless you can prove that someone not only has stolen your number, but that you're experiencing financial harm.

CREDIT-CARD FRAUD

If you suspect or learn for sure that someone is racking up bills on your credit cards or using your credit report to obtain loans, you'll need to contact the fraud departments at each of the three credit-reporting agencies—Equifax, (800) 685-1111; Experian, (888) 397-3742; and TransUnion, (800) 888-4213—and request a free copy of your credit report, as is your right when you suspect fraud. Look the forms over carefully for fraudulent or suspicious accounts. If you find one, go straight to the credit issuer and close the account immediately and then send the creditor a letter disputing the fraudulent account using the sample letter to creditors in Appendix 1 as a guide. Mail only copies—not originals—of all supporting documents, and send the information via certified mail, return-receipt requested. Keep careful files of all your documents, and make a log of any telephone conversations.

After you've dealt with whoever issued the credit, you then should file another dispute letter with the credit-reporting agency, taking issue with any information that you believe is fraudulent. There's a sample letter for that, too, in the Appendix. Also request that each agency place a fraud alert in your file to prevent any new accounts from being opened without your permission. Anyone can request an initial fraud alert, which expires after ninety days unless the consumer requests an extension. Extended fraud alerts stay on the books for seven years. As I've noted earlier, many states now allow residents to request a credit freeze, which may stop companies from extending credit in the consumer's name. That's a good idea as long as you realize that there's some hassle associated with the process since you have to keep up with three separate personal identification numbers and probably pay a fee each time you want to temporarily lift the freeze to obtain credit.

Your next step is to contact your local law-enforcement agency. Ask to file a "miscellaneous incidents" report. Don't expect much in the way of help from your men and women in

RESOURCES FOR QUICK REFERENCE

Social Security Administration
If you suspect Social Security fraud, call or file a complaint online. You should also send a written complaint.

Fraud hotline: (800) 269-0271

www.socialsecurity.gov/oig

SSA Fraud Hotline

P.O. Box 17768

Baltimore, MD 21235

(For state benefits, contact your state labor department. Go to www.dol.gov for contact information.)

Fraud Departments at the Three Major Credit-Reporting Agencies
If you suspect credit-card fraud or that someone has been using your credit report to obtain loans.

Equifax: (800) 685-1111

Experian: (888) 397-3742

TransUnion: (800) 888-4213

Your Local Law-Enforcement Agency
File a "miscellaneous incidents" report. If you find that local police are disinclined to file a report, contact your state police. If you have trouble getting a response, complain to your state attorney general's office.

A listing of offices of state attorneys general can be found online at www.naag.org.

Creditors for All Compromised Accounts
Contact creditors immediately in writing to close all compromised accounts and change all passwords.

The Federal Trade Commission
Call or file a complaint online. You should also mail a copy of your complaint.

FTC's Identity Theft hotline: (887) IDTHEFT (438-4338)

www.consumer.gov/idtheft

Identity Theft Clearinghouse

Federal Trade Commission

600 Pennsylvania Avenue NW

Washington, D.C. 20580

blue—they probably don't have the expertise to do much other than file the report—but you'll want copies of this document to support your claim that you've been the victim of identity theft. If necessary, go to the police station rather than having a police car visit you at home. If the local cops are disinclined to even file a report, contact your state police. And if they won't help—hard to imagine it's this difficult to get help from law enforcement when a crime is committed, but it can be—complain to your state attorney general's office. You can find a list of them at www.naag.org.

It probably won't be any more helpful in getting the perpetrator in jail, but you should also file a complaint with the Federal Trade Commission at www.consumer.gov/idtheft or call the FTC's Identity Theft hotline toll-free at (877) IDTHEFT (438-4338). To mail a copy of your complaint, write to this address: Identity Theft Clearinghouse, Federal Trade Commission, 600 Pennsylvania Avenue NW, Washington, D.C. 20580. The information is entered into the "Consumer Sentinel," a secure database that can be accessed by civil and criminal law-enforcement agencies worldwide. If nothing else, the more people who report identity theft, the more attention it will get from Congress and law-enforcement agencies. I find it encouraging that companies are heeding the call for more accountability. In July, the Identity Theft Assistance Center, a not-for-profit group whose members range from Citigroup to Ford Motor's Ford Motor Credit financial-services unit, announced it would begin sharing information about identity-theft cases with the FTC to help aid law-enforcement officials nationwide.

DRIVER'S LICENSE AND CELL-PHONE FRAUD

If you suspect a criminal has used your information to obtain a driver's license, contact your local Department of Motor Vehicles and ask that your record be flagged for possible fraud. If cell-phone fraud has been detected, contact your local provider and file a complaint with the Federal Communications Commission at www.fcc.gov or call (888) CALL-FCC. You can also write to this address: Federal Communications Commission, Consumer Information Bureau, 445 12th Street, SW, Room 5A863, Washington, D.C. 20554.

Finally, don't let your guard down. The unfortunate fact is that if identity thieves have your Social Security number and other personal information, chances are they'll try to strike again. Be sure to monitor your financial accounts and credit reports carefully for any signs of tampering.

FILING AN IDENTITY-THEFT AFFIDAVIT AND IDENTITY-THEFT REPORT

Once you've notified the lenders and credit-reporting companies that you've become a victim of identity theft and filed a police report to substantiate the crime, you'll be required to provide additional proof to the companies involved that you didn't incur the debt(s) yourself. What type of proof you'll need depends on the crime:

- **For new accounts** opened in your name, you'll have to complete a document called an "ID Theft Affidavit," which is available at http://www.consumer.gov/idtheft/pdf/affidavit.pdf.

- **For existing accounts** with unauthorized charges, you may need an affidavit along with additional supporting documentation (such as police reports, collection agency notifications, etc.).

- **Before submitting any information,** call your creditor's fraud department and find out what information you'll need to provide.

When completing the affidavit and account statements, answer every question as clearly and accurately as possible.

Don't give officials any excuse to sideline your case: Incomplete documents or information that's difficult to read will slow down the investigation of the crime. After completing the affidavit, mail *copies* of it and the supporting documents to each of the companies involved. (Keep all original documents in a safe place.) Many companies require the information within thirty days—delays give identity thieves more time to cover their tracks and hamper creditors' ability to investigate the crime. Again, send the information by certified mail, return-receipt requested, to provide proof of the date the documents were mailed and received.

Remember that providing this information doesn't guarantee you'll catch the criminal or even determine how your identity was stolen. It also doesn't guarantee that the creditors will clear you of responsibility for the fraudulent debt. An ID theft affidavit merely provides creditors with the information they need to investigate the crime and respond to your request for help.

DEALING WITH DEBT COLLECTORS

It would be nice if the steps that I have just listed were guaranteed to get you off the hook for debts fraudulently incurred under your name. It doesn't always work that way. Worse yet, many people discover they've been the victim of identity theft when they get a call or letter from a collection agency.

Robert Sherman of Randolph, New Jersey, tried to convince one distressed-debt buyer that it had the wrong man. In December of 2005, he received a letter from a law firm demanding that he repay $6,200 for an old credit-card debt. Not recognizing the account, he contacted the credit-card company and discovered the account didn't belong to him. When he later applied for a home-equity loan, he learned the fraudulent account appeared on his credit reports.

Collection agency calls can lead to panic and emotional distress—even when you know you didn't incur the debt. If you suspect identity theft, it's *really* time to keep your cool. Collection agencies are aware of the anxiety their calls can generate and they know how to use it to their advantage. Don't let them get the upper hand.

Remember that a collection agency's main goal is to collect on a debt. The collectors don't care whether or not you legitimately owe the money. The important thing here is that the law is on your side: The Fair Debt Collection Practices Act prohibits debt collectors from using unfair or deceptive practices to collect any bills that a creditor has forwarded for collection.

Whether you're contacted by mail or telephone, be careful how you respond to a debt collector. Often collection agencies have scant information beyond a name, account number and the amount owed. You don't need to supply them with any further information over the phone, and a nervous or inappropriate response to a debt collector could potentially give an agency enough evidence to support its argument that you're actually responsible for the debt even when you're not.

The first thing you should do when contacted by phone by any collection agency is to ask for a mailing address where you can send correspondence. Get the agent's name and telephone number, and then tell him or her to stop contacting you by phone and send any correspondence by mail—and then hang up just like that. Immediately make a written record of the call in your log, including the caller's name, telephone number and address. If the agent refused to give that information, your phone's caller ID may retain the number from which the agent was calling. Talking to debt collectors is like speaking to a prosecutor before talking to your lawyer—you may be tricked or persuaded into saying something that down the road could be used against you, making you liable for the debt. By law, within five days of contacting you by phone, the collection agency must send a written notice detailing the amount you owe, the name of the creditor to whom you owe the money and what action to take if you believe you do not owe the money.

A prompt follow-up to that letter is necessary. Send it as soon as possible and not later than thirty days by mailing a letter—certified, return-receipt requested—disputing the debt and demanding that the collection agency stop contacting you. Be sure to make clear that you are disputing the debt. The "Initial Debt Collection Form Letter" in Appendix 1 covers all the legalese for you.

By law, the company can contact you after receiving your letter only to either inform you that there will be no further contact or to let you know if further action is to be taken by the creditor or collection agency. The collector must provide proof of the debt in order to continue collection activities and continue to report the debt to the credit-reporting agencies. Keep a copy of the letter and notes of what was said on the phone call for your records. Generally, a collection agency doesn't want to go to the trouble and expense of pursuing a bad debt through the courts. It's likely that at this point they'll notify you that there will be no further contact.

But some aggressive collectors may press on in the hopes that by getting tougher with you, they'll persuade you to pay the debt just to get them off your back. Unfortunately, not everyone knows that harassing or threatening phone calls, the use of foul language and calls threatening legal action or repossession are among the numerous acts prohibited by law. If you get those kinds of calls, inform the caller that his or her actions are in violation of the law and that you intend to report the call to the authorities. Keep a log of any such calls, including the date and time of day, the name of the person calling you and anything you find threatening or offensive. If you have evidence of violations, you can sue a collector within one year from the date the law was violated. Once you threaten to take them to court, they typically leave you alone and move on to consumers with less backbone. But if you do sue and win, you could receive up to $1,000 per action, along with court costs and your attorney's fees.

If the collection agency sends you what it purports to be documentation that you owe the debt, immediately contact the three main credit-reporting companies—Experian, Equifax and TransUnion—to dispute any account information you suspect to be incorrect or fraudulent. The credit bureaus will then contact the debt buyer and demand documentation to prove the account is valid. If the debt buyer can't provide sufficient proof, the account will be removed from your credit report. Also, file a complaint with the FTC at www.ftc.gov or call (877) 382-4357. If the collection agency is mailing false or misleading documentation or correspondence, inform the U.S. Postal Service of possible mail fraud.

WHERE TO LOOK FOR MORE HELP

Sometimes it helps to have someone working with you to recover from identity theft. More companies have begun offering help for victims in the workplace. For example, some large companies now offer identity-theft insurance and recovery services to their employees as part of their benefits packages to help workers cut down on lost time. If you've been a victim of identity theft, check with your company's human resources office to see if help is available. Insurance companies also offer individual policies to help victims pay legal expenses when fighting back from an identity theft. A number of insurers now offer identity-theft insurance riders to homeowners' insurance policies.

In fact, in recent years a cottage industry has sprung up to help victims recover from identity theft, although the quality and value of the services offered vary widely. Most are designed to alert you quickly if fraud is suspected and help you manage the long hours and detective work necessary to reclaim your good name. Valuable services handle the paperwork for you and act as go-betweens with creditors and collection agencies.

So-called identity-theft restoration services that provide little more than a "how-to" manual to follow in the event of a crime generally aren't worth the cost. These services can help with paperwork and provide emotional support, but there are limits on what they can do:

- If a credit-reporting company has investigated the victim's claim and determined that the information on the report isn't fraudulent, there isn't anything the victim or the resolution company can do to remove the information from his or her credit history, even if he or she is sure it's wrong.

- Police reports, which are essential in proving to creditors and government agencies that you've become a victim of identity theft, can be filed only by victims. Some services will contact your local police and make them aware that you're coming and will provide you with the documentation to help prove a theft has taken place.

- Government agencies, such as the Social Security Administration or your local Division of Motor Vehicles, generally are unwilling to deal with third parties without a power of attorney.

If you're considering hiring one of these services, ask what the company would specifically require you to do in the event that you become a victim and what recovery services it would provide. Find out if the company provides recovery insurance or any kind of monetary guarantee should you become a victim while a client of the service. Get specifics on which costs would be covered and which would not—is it just postage expenses and phone calls that would be covered, or would legal bills and reimbursement for time off from work also be covered? Then decide on your own whether the service is worth the cost.

STOPPING HARASSMENT FROM IDENTITY THIEVES

Remember that I talked earlier about how some people steal a person's identity in order to harass that person by assuming the victim's identity on the Internet and doing or saying things that invite ridicule or scorn? Such tricksters are often kids who want to embarrass a particular schoolmate. If someone is posing online as either you or your child, you can try to track down the perpetrator at http://www.whois.com. By typing in the name of the Web site, you can find out who paid for it. You can also have e-mails and instant messages, which are sometimes the weapon of choice among harassers, traced through screen names and addresses provided by the Internet service provider. It may take some time and effort, but you may be able to find the person or group of people behind the harassment. Parents who make such a discovery should contact their child's school principal immediately to discuss the bullying. Adults who are being targeted should file a complaint with the local police department and consider hiring an attorney to issue a cease-and-desist letter.

COMBATING CRIMINAL VIOLATIONS

It's upsetting enough to find that an identity thief has been using your information to open lines of credit and make fraudulent purchases. But what if you discover someone has been out there using your information to impersonate you and commit crimes in your name? How shocked would you be if you were pulled over for a minor traffic violation and suddenly found yourself under arrest and charged with a serious crime you know you didn't commit? The fact that you're wanted for a crime might come to light in other, perhaps less-frightening ways, such as being turned down for a lease on an apartment or for a new job as a result of a background check that revealed crimes committed by someone else in your name. While that wouldn't be as awful as being arrested and dragged off to jail, it's still bad news.

If you discover that an impersonator has committed crimes in your name, contact the police or sheriff's office that either arrested the impersonator or issued the warrant for the arrest. Most law-enforcement departments will allow you to file an impersonation report and to confirm your identity. But brace yourself! This isn't going to be fun and you'll begin to get a sense of how frightening the criminal justice system is. Law-enforcement officials may require you to be fingerprinted and photographed, and they may have copies made of your picture identification, such as a driver's license, passport or work ID.

If the arrest warrant is from a state or county far from where you live, ask the local police to send the impersonation report to the police department in the jurisdiction where the offense originated.

After you've established the theft of your identity (and your innocence), the police should recall any outstanding warrants and issue a "clearance letter" or "certificate of release" in the event you actually had been arrested and booked for a crime. Keep this document with you at all times in case you're wrongly arrested again. Make sure your local law enforcers follow up with the police department or district attorney's office in the jurisdiction where the crime took place to corroborate your innocence. To avoid future confusion should your name pop up on the criminal database, ask that the "primary name" on the complaint be changed from your name to the real criminal's name. If the criminal is unknown, ask to have it changed to "John Doe" or "Jane Doe," with your name noted only as an alias.

Clearing your name on court documents and law-enforcement databases can be a much stickier proposition if your state has no formal procedure in place in the event of identity theft. Until you correct your information in the system, you may be vulnerable to arrest and other consequences, such as losing your job or finding yourself unable to obtain credit. When serious criminal offenses have been committed in your name, I strongly recommend that you obtain legal counsel to help you navigate the system and avoid being arrested.

If you're accused of a criminal offense as a result of identity theft, find a defense attorney by contacting your local bar association or searching for a lawyer at the Web site of the American Bar Association at www.abanet.org/legalservices/findlegalhelp. Some states also permit criminal records to be sealed or expunged, a legal process more complicated than simply showing up at the local police station and corroborating your identity. Your attorney will complete all necessary forms and file a petition on your behalf with the court to have your criminal records sealed or expunged.

CHAPTER 7

EASING THE EMOTIONAL PAIN

Together with me now: Breathe.

Recovering from the emotional toll of identity theft can be one of the most stressful ordeals you'll ever experience. Month after month, you live with the feeling of dread and fear, wondering what new bill will show up in the mail or when the next collection agency will call. In severe cases, you may be facing a run-in with the law, resulting in the terrifying possibility of arrest or incarceration. The stress you're feeling is perfectly normal—you'd be crazy if you didn't have these feelings.

Perhaps no case better illustrates the emotional roller coaster victims endure than what happened to Eric Drew. In December 2002, Drew received a devastating diagnosis—while donating blood to the American Red Cross, it was discovered that he had a life-threatening leukemia. Deeply depressed after months of debilitating and sometimes fruitless chemotherapy and radiation treatments, he received more distressing news. A debt-collection agency contacted him about an overdue credit account that he had never opened. When he told the agency he must be a victim of identity theft, the callous agent recommended he pay the bill off and file a dispute with the credit-reporting agency to avoid having the past-due amount damage his credit score.

Drew later found that a hospital worker—believing Drew was about to die—stole his personal information and used a number of credit-card accounts to buy diamonds, Christmas gifts, camping gear and other pricey items. Enraged at the injustice, Drew managed to sum up the strength to track the thief down, and with the help of media outlets detailing his story, he had the thief prosecuted under the federal Health Insurance Portability and Accountability Act—the first prosecution ever under the act. It's mind-boggling to think about a man struggling to track down and reclaim his own identity from what he feared might have been his deathbed.

While most victims' circumstances are nowhere near as dire as Drew's, the emotional toll of identity theft can be demoralizing, with effects that can linger long after victims are made whole again financially.

A 2003 report by the San Diego–based Identity Theft Resource Center found that victims spend an average of six hundred hours recovering from identity theft, equivalent to roughly $16,000 in lost income. While victims are finding out about the crimes more quickly than they had in the past, the survey found that they're nevertheless suffering in more ways than ever before. Victims surveyed reported an emotional toll similar to those reporting rape or other kinds of violent crime. Some said they felt dirty, defiled, ashamed and embarrassed and undeserving of assistance. The study found that some victims reported splitting up with significant others who were unable or unwilling to deal with the aftermath of the crime.

Depending on the extent of the crime, victims' reactions can range from constant anxiety to dread of the sound of a phone ringing to frustration with the organizations that should be working with them—not against them—to resolve the matter to sheer panic at the realization that there may be a warrant out for their arrest. These feelings can be compounded in cases in which victims learn that the people responsible for the theft are friends, family members or coworkers. Learning how to cope with these roiling emotions can be the most difficult part of the recovery process.

According to the National Organization for Victim Assistance (NOVA) in Alexandria, Virginia, the financial losses suffered by victims of identity theft are just one of four types of injuries victims of crime must endure. The physical symptoms that accompany identity theft—stress, anxiety, head and stomach aches and insomnia are just a few of the common reactions to becoming a victim of a crime—often are endured in silence. NOVA says victims can also suffer socially, when spouses, friends or coworkers fail to provide support and understanding while the victims attempt to recover from the crime.

My initial reaction to discovering I'd become a victim of identity theft was shock and anger. How could someone have gained access to my credit-card number when the card was sitting right there in my wallet? But that was nothing compared to the anxiety and sense of dread I felt afterward, fearful that the thief would strike again. For months, I obsessively checked my financial accounts online, sometimes more than once a day, nervously on the lookout for any suspicious activity. I closed several credit-card accounts I had kept open for years (but never used) to ease the stress of worrying whether a thief might take advantage of an account I wasn't monitoring very closely. That sense of unease has lessened over the years as I've become more aggressive in keeping a close eye on my family's credit reports and financial accounts. But the dread I feel knowing that my personal information is out there lingers to this day. These are all common feelings shared by identity-theft victims.

COMING BACK

The first stage in rebounding emotionally from identity theft is to recognize that you're a victim of a crime and that it's perfectly reasonable for you to have feelings of fear, anger, embarrassment, mistrust and frustration. Over the next few weeks or months, you may feel bogged down in the process of document-ing the theft and clearing your name. You may discover that in addition to the loss of innocence you feel in discovering you've become a victim, you'll also feel a sense of disillusionment as you deal with companies and law-enforcement officials who should be on your side, but often don't seem to be. In worst-case scenarios, you may suffer physical and emotional prob-lems, such as chronic headaches or depression.

If you're a victim, it's important to find ways to manage your anxiety and avoid other sources of stress in your life. First, you need to recognize the signs of stress: Shallow breathing, dry mouth, stammering, trouble sleeping, a feeling of tightness in your chest, tense muscles and headaches are all common symptoms. Excessive irritability and an inability to concentrate or focus on completing a task are other warning signs of stress.

At the start of this chapter, I wasn't joking when I urged you to breathe—stress often causes you to hold your breath or to breathe shallowly, increasing tension in your body and lead-ing to even more stress. One of the easiest ways to decompress from stress is to find some quiet time for yourself and breathe deeply. Exercise is another great stress-buster. Take all that anger, frustration and anxiety and funnel it into a daily work-out. Now is also the time to re-evaluate your diet—eating bet-ter will release toxins from your body and give you the strength you'll need to face each day. Try signing up for a yoga or med-itation class or schedule regular visits to the spa for massage and other restorative treatments. Simply stepping away from your desk to take a relaxing walk in a park can give your mind a much-needed mini-vacation from the typical day-to-day stresses of the office. In extreme cases of depression, you may want to consider taking time off from your job to work with a professional to deal with your emotions. By doing all of these things, you'll ease tension in your body and enjoy the benefits of leading a healthier lifestyle.

Are you the absent-minded type? Quick to lose your keys, forget appointments or miss bill-payment due dates? Now is the perfect time to work on those issues, because the stress of becoming a victim will only make your bad habits worse. Start planning ahead and making lists of things you need to do each day. Schedule your time, hour-by-hour, and be generous when allocating how long certain tasks will take. Allocating a half-hour to run one or two errands may require more time than that if traffic is heavy or store checkout lines are long. Getting behind in your schedule will only add to your stress. And be sure to allocate time to spend just on taking care of you.

Talking to family or friends about your feelings can also help to reduce stress. They may not be able to help you recover from the crime, but they can provide some emotional support and let you know that you're not suffering through it alone. But do try to avoid overloading your loved ones with your problems. If family members or friends attempt to change the subject when you try to discuss your feelings, it may be time to seek a professional counselor. Another great way to vent your feelings is to keep a diary, which also creates a helpful daily log of your struggle to reclaim your identity.

While some doctors prescribe medicines to help victims overcome their depression and anxiety, avoid the impulse to medicate yourself using over-the-counter products such as herbal remedies and sleeping pills. The urge to self-medicate by turning to alcohol or drugs or resuming smoking may also be strong, but these are impulses you need to overcome. If you feel incapable of managing your stress alone, contact your doctor.

Finally, I don't know about you, but for me, nothing releases frustration and anxiety faster than having a good cry. I know big boys and tough girls aren't supposed to cry, but you men shouldn't discount the ability of a good cry to ease tension and clear your mind. There's nothing wrong with finding some time for yourself and just letting all the emotions flow out with your tears. That said, if you find yourself crying all of the time, make an appointment to see your doctor—you could be suffering from depression.

Victims who discover the crime was committed by someone

they know have a whole different set of feelings to contend with. You may at first feel outrage, betrayal and disappointment, but at the same time pity and reluctance to bring criminal charges against the family member or friend. In fact, many identity thieves become brazen enough to commit crimes because they assume that the family member or friend won't prosecute. Some relatives may also put pressure on you to resolve the issue within the family, particularly in cases involving relatively minor offenses. For example, a brother steals your information to apply for a driver's license in your name after having his own license revoked for drunk driving. Or a father uses his child's identity to open a cell phone account because his own credit is so bad that he can't open one of his own.

When the theft involves smaller crimes, victims should first consider whether it's worth the emotional toll of bringing charges against the thief. Do you really need the stress of being dragged through the court system in addition to handling all of the work necessary to recover from the crime? The payoff is likely to be unsatisfying; for petty crimes, it's unlikely the thief will get much jail time. Law-enforcement officials know this and in many cases won't bother to follow up after the crime has been reported. In these situations, it may be better to simply forgive the thief. Forgive, but don't forget! Work on recovering any losses you may have suffered and then take the steps outlined in this book to prevent the criminal from impersonating you again. Also make sure the thief knows that you've documented the crime and that you *will* prosecute if he or she once again impersonates you for any reason.

Victims who are less willing to forgive a family member or friend or who are having a harder time moving on with their lives may want to consider family counseling to help heal the wounds. Ideally, victim and thief would meet together to acknowledge the crime and attempt to resolve hurt feelings and begin to work together at rebuilding trust. If that's not an option, consider attending counseling with other family members who were affected by the crime. It can be cathartic just to have the people you love acknowledge your feelings and the fortitude it takes to turn the other cheek for the sake of family. As a last resort, go see a counselor on your own to come to terms with your feelings and why you're having trouble forgiving the criminal and moving on with your life.

In extreme cases, however, the best route may be to either report the person to law-enforcement officials or seek an attorney for help in recovering your losses. Be forewarned: The emotional ramifications can tear families apart. One column I'd written about identity theft a few years ago elicited a memorable letter from an Online Journal reader whose family was in upheaval after the victim turned her mother in to the police for using her personal information to open up numerous credit-card accounts. The daughter discovered the crime after being turned down for a mortgage because her credit score was so low. After her mother's arrest, her brothers and sisters took sides—one side backing the victim's decision and the other side furious with her for airing the family's dirty laundry in public. After making the devastatingly difficult decision to turn her own mother in to the police, she and the siblings who supported her were ostracized by half of her family. Though she felt she was doing the right thing at the time, she now lives with feelings of sadness and regret that she was responsible for the family breaking up. In cases such as this, there may be nothing you can do to prevent hurt feelings. Remember that what's most important is your own mental well-being, not your family's discomfort or embarrassment.

For some victims of identity theft, the trauma of recovering from the crime can have devastating effects on their health. Take John Harrison, a retired Army Captain. He suffered debilitating trauma after he learned that in 2001, a thief had acquired an active duty military identity card on which his name and Social Security number were printed. He discovered the crime after a police officer from another state contacted him about a stolen Harley Davidson motorcycle. The person pulled over riding the Harley, Jerry Wayne Phillips, showed the police officer the active duty military ID with Harrison's name on it. Some quick detective work led police officials to contact Harrison and notify him of the crime. Harrison later found that the thief had used the card to open more than sixty fraudulent checking and credit-card accounts and to obtain several loans. Phillips served some jail time for his crimes, but Harrison would suffer an even worse fate. After spending eleven months attempting to clear his name—often repeatedly having to deal with the same companies who continued to open accounts and extend credit to the thief—Harrison began to suffer from anxiety and insomnia. His doctor prescribed antidepressants and ultimately he was diagnosed with depression and post-traumatic stress disorder.

Some identity-theft victims, like John Harrison, need professional help to cope with their recovery. If you or a family member notice severe changes in your personal behavior— insomnia, fatigue, exhaustion, abusing alcohol or sleeping pills—it's time to reach out for help. Your doctor or clergyman can recommend local mental-health support groups, and many employers offer mental-health programs as part of their employee-assistance programs. Also, check with your local hospital for access to government-sponsored mental-health clinics or support groups.

You've already taken a strong first step in your healing process by reading this book. Using all the tools available to you to monitor your accounts and credit reports and documenting your journey toward clearing your name can be empowering. I know, I've been there. In fact, many victims of identity theft find that clearing their own name isn't enough; they reach out to the growing number of identity-theft advocacy groups that are fighting for tougher laws and stricter regulation of the financial-services and credit-reporting industries. You can find a list of local advocacy groups in your area or find all the information you need to start an advocacy group of your own by calling the Identity Theft Resource Center in San

Diego at (858) 693-7935 or e-mailing the group at itrc@idtheft center.org.

There are also a number of victim assistance programs that may help in your recovery efforts. Victim assistance programs often offer free counseling and compensation for lost earnings related to recovering from the theft. The quickest way to find one in your area is to ask your local law-enforcement agency if it sponsors this type of program. If crimes have been committed in your name, you can also contact your local prosecutor's office and ask to speak to a victims' advocate, who can help you through the process as your case is investigated.

If no victim support programs are available to you, you may be referred to a community-based program in your area. To locate a community-based victim assistance program on your own, call NOVA's toll-free National Crime Victim Information and Referral hotline at (800) 879-6682. You may also find community-based programs in your phone book under the "community services" section. Finally, you can find additional resources to help you cope at identity-theft victims' rights organizations such as the San Diego–based Identity Theft Resource Center (online at www.idtheftcenter.org or call (858) 693-7935) or the Privacy Rights Clearinghouse (www.privacy rights.org).

Identity-theft victims typically go through an extremely trying time as they struggle to reclaim their identities. The very thought that someone out there has impersonated you to commit crimes—and could potentially do it again—is traumatizing. Listen to your body's signals and pamper yourself when you need it. And don't be afraid or embarrassed to reach out for professional help if you need it.

CHAPTER 8

IDENTITY THEFT IN POP CULTURE

Just twenty years ago, it seemed like identity theft was a remote crime that had little impact on Americans' daily lives. Oh, how times have changed. Today, identity theft and the havoc it can cause have made their way into pop culture. From television shows and movies to books, music and the Internet, identity theft permeates our way of life. In this chapter, we'll look at some of the frightening and funny ways identity theft has been portrayed in pop culture.

As disgusting and upsetting as identity theft is when we're the victims, it's surprisingly easy to shift gears entirely and see scamsters on the big screen as lovable and even as heroes. The light-hearted 2002 movie *Catch Me If You Can*, starring Leonardo DiCaprio, follows the life of Frank Abagnale Jr., a real-life teenage identity thief who managed to cash more than $2.5 million in fraudulent checks in twenty-six countries in the 1960s. Along the way, Abagnale successfully impersonated all kinds of respected individuals, from a doctor and an airline pilot to an assistant attorney general. Actor Tom Hanks portrayed Carl Hanratty, an FBI agent who doggedly pursued the teenage con artist.

But the movies can depict ID theft in grim terms, too. In 1995, a movie starring Sandra Bullock revealed the very real terror and sense of helplessness that grips victims whose identities come into question. In *The Net,* the actress stars as Angela Bennett, a computer programmer who discovers that all of her personal records—credit cards, bank accounts and driver's license—are gone. In their place, she's been given a whole new identity (one that comes with a police record) by agents who are attempting to recover a computer disk she'd been given with secret information on it. The thriller detailed many of the difficulties and emotional real-life traumas identity victims face in trying to reclaim their good names.

Nearly ten years later, Michelle Brown's harrowing real-life experience at the hands of a prolific identity thief struck such a chord that it eventually led her to testify at a hearing before a Senate committee. The Hermosa Beach, California, woman had her name and Social Security number stolen from an apartment-rental application. The identity thief proceeded to use Ms. Brown's name and Social Security number to purchase over $50,000 worth of goods and services including an automobile, phone service, utilities, store credit cards and even a liposuction procedure. She also later discovered that a warrant had been issued for her arrest on drug-smuggling charges brought against the woman who had stolen her identity.

Brown's testimony so moved California Senator Dianne Feinstein that she introduced legislation to toughen penalties for identity-theft offenses. The bill was passed and signed into law, and Brown's story was told in the 2004 TV movie *Identity Theft: The Michelle Brown Story.*

In the 2001 film *The Familiar Stranger,* a father indicted for embezzlement fakes his own death and runs out on his family, taking on a new identity. His wife, suspicious that her husband may still be alive, uses every online resource available to her to track her husband down and make him pay for his sins.

Many books, plays and films focus on imposters posing as other people for personal gain. 1993's *Six Degrees of Separation* and 1999's *The Talented Mr. Ripley* are both movies in which characters pose as other people to gain a foothold in high society. *Six Degrees of Separation,* a play and film written by John Guare, was inspired by the real-life story of David Hampton, an artist who famously conned a wealthy group of New York City socialites after convincing them he was the son of actor Sidney Poitier. Prior to that, Hampton managed to con a number of high-profile celebrities and professionals into giving him money or letting him stay at their homes by posing as a friend of the family he was conning.

In *The Talented Mr. Ripley,* based on the 1955 novel by Patricia Highsmith, the character Tom Ripley is a poor man who pretends to be a friend of a wealthy man's son. After gaining Herbert Greenleaf's confidence, he urges Ripley to travel to Italy to persuade the son to return to New York. Ripley later murders the son and assumes his identity, living an opulent lifestyle financed by the dead man's unsuspecting father. In the end, Ripley forges Herbert Greenleaf's will and ends up inheriting the dead son's fortune.

The book's tale was eerily mirrored almost a decade later when real-life drifter Fabio Pereira was convicted of the murder of London millionaire John Goodman. Pereira, an illegal immigrant from Brazil, murdered Goodman and then immediately moved into his apartment and began impersonating him, spending lavishly from his bank accounts and credit cards until a police investigation led to his conviction for murder and obtaining property by deception.

In season six of the trend-setting Home Box Office cable TV series *Sex and the City,* the character Samantha steals the entry card of a person named Annabelle Bronstein who's a member of an elite spa in order to gain access to its roof-top pool. She keeps posing as Bronstein until the real Bronstein is discovered, and Samantha and her guests are all forced to leave the pool in embarrassment.

Nowhere is the use of stolen identities and fraudulent documentation more prevalent than in television shows, books and movies on espionage. Most recently, the franchise hit *The Bourne Identity*, which was loosely based on Robert Ludlum's novel of the same name, featured themes involving identity. In *The Bourne Identity* and its sequels, *The Bourne Supremacy* and the upcoming *The Bourne Ultimatum*, actor Matt Damon plays Jason Bourne, a man with amnesia who discovers a bank vault in his name that holds numerous passports with his picture—all in different names. He later discovers that he was a former agent with the Central Intelligence Agency.

Occasionally, writers and producers take a more light-hearted approach to the issue of identity theft, often revealing truths about ourselves along the way. Woody Allen's 1983 film *Zelig* took a comedic look at impersonators. Allen played Leonard Zelig, a man who has the chameleon-like ability to change his appearance and manner of speech to reflect that of the people he stands close to. Allen's ex Mia Farrow played a psychiatrist who discovers Zelig's desperate need for approval is behind his odd condition.

No television show is more on the cutting-edge of pop culture these days than *The Daily Show*, a news-parody show on the cable television channel Comedy Central. After a spate of highly publicized cases of identity theft, the show featured one segment titled "Digital Watch," in which technology reporter Ed Helms offers "tips" on how to avoid identity theft like this one: "Don't ever use e-mail, ever! Do what normal people do and call your friends and family on the phone, for God's sake!" The faux reporter also accidentally gives out his password and notes that someone has accessed his checking account and emptied it.

It wasn't the first time identity theft has been parodied on TV. In one amusing episode of the animated series *The Simpsons,* character Seymour Skinner, the long-time principal of Springfield Elementary school, is revealed by the real Seymour Skinner to be an imposter named Armen Tamzarian. The two met during their military service in the Army, and Tamzarian even-tually traveled to Springfield to tell Skinner's mother that Skin-ner had been killed even though he wasn't. After Tamzarian admits he's a fraud and leaves town in shame, the townspeople realize they prefer the fake Skinner to the real thing. The Simpson family manages to lure Tamzarian back to Springfield and runs the real Skinner out of town.

One of my favorite identity-theft news parodies appeared in *The Onion,* a newspaper and Web site that always manages to find the humor that lurks in the day's most troubling head-lines. In its May 4, 2005, edition, *The Onion* tackled identity theft with this news item:

> WASHINGTON, DC—Confusion and disbelief reigned at the White House after President Bush announced Monday that an Arizona man, known to authorities only as H4xX0r1337, stole his identity and used it to buy electronic goods, veto a bill, and meet with Mexican President Vicente Fox.
>
> "This is incredibly frustrating," Bush told reporters Tues-day. "Not only does this guy have my credit-card information, he has my Social Security number, all my personal information, and the launch codes for a number of ballistic intercontinen-tal nuclear missiles. I almost don't want to think about it.
>
> "I feel so violated," Bush added.

The fake news article goes on to explain how the president fell victim to a "phishing scam" when he responded to a fraud-ulent e-mail claiming to be from financial Web site PayPal ask-ing him to provide credit-card numbers, his Social Security number and all of his passwords and PINs.

It's a hilarious send-up, but not that far off course—con-sumers fall victim to this kind of scam all the time, providing sensitive personal and financial information to thieves posing as legitimate companies.

Humorist Dave Barry also took on the issue of identity theft in his 2005 year-end review. In his column, Barry noted that "as the nationwide identity-theft epidemic worsens, FBI Director Robert S. Mueller III pledges that he will make it the top priority of the Bureau to find, and prosecute, the individuals charging stuff to his American Express card."

Recently Citibank turned the problem of identity theft on its head by having actors portray unsuspecting victims of identity theft in television commercials promoting its Citi Identity Theft Solutions victim-support service. The spots featured average-looking people, but when they spoke, their voices were clearly not their own. Instead, the voices were intended to be those of the identity thieves who were using their credit cards to make fraudulent purchases. One spot featured an older man, who spoke in a voice that clearly belonged to a young girl, boasting about how she used his money to buy a $1,500 leather bustier. The commercials were funny and memorable and hopefully opened the audiences' eyes to the real threat of identity theft.

One form of popular conversation bringing people together to discuss identity theft online is the launch of myriad Web logs, or "blogs." Bloggers post their comments about the latest news and research involving identity theft, help keep people up to date on the latest developments and challenge readers to share their views on the crime.

Identity Theft Blog by Truston had a great example of a blog post that brings together information to tell a larger story about how companies and organizations are failing to secure laptops carrying sensitive consumer information. An August 26,

Among the blogs that I routinely check for news and information on the latest identity-theft scams and privacy-protection technology are the following.

- **Technorati**
  (http://www.technorati.com/tags/identitytheft)

- **FightIdentityTheft blog**
  (http://www.fightidentitytheft.com/blog)

- **Schneier on Security**
  (http://www.schneier.com/blog)

- **Identity Theft Blog by Truston**
  (http://www.mytruston.com/blog)

2006, post tracking data breaches involving laptops noted the following.

These are just the incidents *that we know* of thus far in *August 2006.*

- August 26: Sovereign Bank has 3 laptops stolen, customer data lost.

- August 25: U.S. Dept. of Transportation, a laptop stolen that might have sensitive data on 200 people.

- August 25: Dominion Resources, two laptops stolen with employee data.

- August 22: Beaumont Hospital, laptop stolen from car with data on 28,000 patients.

- August 22: AFLAC, laptop stolen with data on 600 policy holders.

- August 17: Williams-Sonoma, laptop stolen from home of Deloitte employee, with data on 1200 employees.

- August 16: Chevron had a laptop stolen with unknown amount of compromised employee data.

- August 15: U.S. Dept. of Transportation, laptop stolen from hotel conference room.

- August 9: U.S. Dept. of Transportation, laptop stolen from government vehicle, with data on 130,000 people.

- August 4: PSA HealthCare, laptop stolen from a contractor, data on 51,000 patients on it.

- August 4: Toyota, laptop stolen from employee's car in their parking lot.

The blogger used information gathered from the Privacy Rights Clearinghouse in addition to his own research. With so many organizations reporting lost or stolen consumer data, the news media turns its attention to these security breaches only when the loss is egregious—such as the laptop with information on roughly 26.5 million people that was stolen from the Veterans Administration. But as this post shows, sensitive information on tens of thousands of people is being breached each month, and the losses are largely going unreported.

The one area where identity theft has yet to creep into our consciousness is in music and radio. There are relatively few odes to the crime, and bands that allude to identity theft are usually referring to their journeys to find their identities rather than having them co-opted. For instance, one recent album by the rock band Enation titled *Identity Theft* focuses on the quest of individuals to find their way in life at a time when so many children are being raised without fathers.

The treatment that identity theft gets in the movies and books and on television leaves me with two conclusions. First and unfortunately, it's here to stay. It's too easy and too lucrative and will continue to attract people looking to make an easy buck at your expense. Second and somewhat more encouraging, the attention the subject is getting invariably heightens awareness of how common the crime is, and that, I hope, will put more people on the defensive, guarding against becoming victims.

SAMPLE LETTERS FOR DEALING WITH IDENTITY THEFT

Sample Letter Reporting Fraudulent or Suspicious Information on Your Credit Report

This letter can be used to notify the three major credit-reporting agencies that you have detected fraudulent or suspicious accounts on one of your credit reports (see pages 63–64). You should also request that fraud alerts be placed in your files to prevent new accounts from being opened without your permission. Anyone can request an initial fraud alert, which expires after ninety days unless the consumer requests an extension. Extended fraud alerts stay on the books for seven years. Many states now allow residents to also request a credit freeze, which may stop companies from extending credit in the consumer's name. But stay vigilant—some creditors ignore fraud alerts altogether.

Your Name   Date
Your Address
Your Telephone Number

Complaint Department
Name of Consumer Reporting Company
Address

Dear Sir or Madam:

I am a victim of identity theft. I am writing to request that you block the following fraudulent information in my file. This information does not relate to any transaction that I have made. The items also are circled on the attached copy of the credit report I received. [Identify item(s) to be blocked by name of source, such as creditors or tax court, and identify type of item, such as credit account, judgment, etc.]

Enclosed is a copy of the law-enforcement report regarding my identity theft. Please let me know if you need any other information from me to block this information on my credit report.

Sincerely,
Your Name
Enclosures: (List what you are enclosing.)

Source: Federal Trade Commission

Sample Letter Notifying Creditors About Compromised Accounts

Use this letter to close all accounts that have been compromised by thieves (see page 133). Don't forget to change passwords, too. Contact creditors immediately to dispute fraudulent accounts. Mail only copies—not originals—of all supporting documents, and send the information via certified mail, return-receipt requested. Keep careful files of all your documents, and make a log of any telephone conversations.

Your Name   Date
Your Address
Your Telephone Number
Your Account Number

Name of Creditor
Billing Inquiries
Address

Dear Sir or Madam:

I am writing to dispute a fraudulent [charge or debit] on my account in the amount of $____. I am a victim of identity theft, and I did not make this [charge or debit]. I am requesting that the [charge be removed or the debit reinstated], that any finance and other charges related to the fraudulent amount be credited and that I receive an accurate statement.

Enclosed are copies of [use this sentence to describe any enclosed information, such as a police report] supporting my position. Please investigate this matter and correct the fraudulent [charge or debit] as soon as possible.

Sincerely,
Your Name
Enclosures: (List what you are enclosing.)

Source: Federal Trade Commission

Sample Letter to Stop Collection Agency Harassment

The following letter can be used under the Fair Debt Collection Practices Act to stop debt collectors from using harassment or unfair or deceptive practices to collect any bills that a creditor has forwarded for collection (see page 137). You'll doubtless be surprised when you get a telephone call or letter from a debt-collection agency, but you must remember to be careful how you respond to a debt collector.

The first thing you should do when contacted by phone by any collection agency is to ask for a mailing address where you can send correspondence. Then tell the agent to stop contacting you by phone and send any correspondence by mail—and then hang up. Period.

By law, within five days of contacting you by phone, the collection agency must send a written notice detailing the amount you owe, the name of the creditor to whom you owe the money and what action to take if you believe you do not owe the money.

Follow up within thirty days by mailing a letter—send it via certified mail, return-receipt requested—disputing the debt and demanding that the collection agency stop contacting you. Be sure to make clear that you are disputing the debt. This sample letter handles all of the legalese for you.

Your Name   Date
Your Address
Your Telephone Number

Name of Collector
Address

Dear Sir or Madam:

I am writing in response to your [letter dated—provide date; or, phone call on—provide date] (copy enclosed) because I don't believe I am responsible for this debt.

This is the first I've heard from you or any other company on this matter. Therefore, in accordance with the Fair Debt Collection Practices Act, Section 809(b): Validating Debts:

(b) If the consumer notifies the debt collector in writing within the thirty-day period described in subsection (a) that the debt, or any portion thereof, is disputed, or that the consumer requests the name and address of the original creditor, the debt collector shall cease collection of the debt, or any disputed portion thereof, until the debt collector obtains verification of the debt or any copy of a judgment, or the name and address of the original creditor, and a copy of such verification or judgment, or name and address of the original creditor, is mailed to the consumer by the debt collector.

I respectfully request that you provide me with the following information:

(1) the amount of the debt you claim I owe;

(2) the name of the creditor to whom the debt is owed;

(3) verification or copy of any judgment [if applicable]; and

(4) proof that you are licensed to collect debts in [insert name of your state].

Be advised that I am fully aware of my rights under the Fair Debt Collection Practices Act and the Fair Credit Reporting Act. For instance, I know the following:

• because I have disputed this debt in writing within thirty days of receipt of your dunning notice, you must obtain verification of the debt or a copy of the judgment against me and mail these items to me at your expense;

• you cannot add interest or fees except those allowed by the original contract or state law; and

• you do not have to respond to this dispute, but if you do, any attempt to collect this debt without validating it violates the FDCPA.

Also be advised that I am keeping very accurate records of all correspondence from you and your company, including recording all phone calls. I will not hesitate to report violations of the law to my state attorney general, the Federal Trade Commission and the Better Business Bureau.

I have disputed this debt. Therefore, until validated, you know that your information concerning this debt is inaccurate. Thus, if you have already reported this debt to any credit-reporting agency or credit bureau, you must immediately inform them of my dispute with this debt. Reporting information that you know to be inaccurate or failing to report information correctly violates the Fair Credit Reporting Act §1681s-2. Should you pursue a judgment without validating this debt, I will inform the judge and request the case be dismissed based on your failure to comply with the FDCPA.

Finally, if you do not own this debt, I demand that you immediately send a copy of this dispute letter to the original creditor so it is also aware of my dispute with this debt.

Sincerely,
Your Name

Sample Letter to Dispute Fraudulent Bankruptcy Petition

This sample letter can be used if you discover an imposter has filed a bankruptcy petition in your name (see page 44). It should be sent to the U.S. Trustee where the petition was filed. A list of the U.S. Trustee Programs' Regional Offices is available at http://www.usdoj.gov/ust/eo/ust_org/office_map.htm. You can also find listings for regional offices in the blue pages of your phone book under "U.S. Government Bankruptcy Administration."

Your letter should indicate that you are a victim of identity theft, provide proof of your identity and describe how you discovered the bankruptcy petition fraudulently filed in your name. Before you send the letter—certified mail, return-receipt requested—file a police report with your local law-enforcement agency and complete an Identity-Theft Affidavit (see below). Include copies of these documents, along with copies of photo identification (your driver's license or work ID) and a few other documents that help establish your identity, such as a U.S. passport, military ID or utility bill. Finally, go to the court where the petition was filed and request copies of the court documents relating to the filing. Remember, send copies! Keep all originals relating to the crime together with you for future reference.

Your Name   Date
Your Address
Your Telephone Number

Clerk of the [County Name] Superior Court
Address
Name(s) of Creditor Attorneys
Address
Re: [Your Name, Your Case #]

Dear Sir or Madam:

It has come to my attention that there is a case [or judgment] against me that was filed in your court. I am a victim of identity theft and in no way am I involved in this case [or judgment].

To establish my identity, I have enclosed copies of my [types of documents you provide as evidence of your identity], a copy of a police report detailing the crime, a copy of a Federal Trade Commission Identity-Theft Affidavit and copies of the court documents involving this case [or judgment].

I became aware of this case [or judgment] on [date you discovered the petition], when I [describe how you discovered the petition: checked my credit report, was denied credit, etc.].

Please advise me how to proceed to get this case dismissed [or this judgment expunged] and whether it is necessary for me to hire an attorney to assist in the process. I would also greatly appreciate any guidance I can receive from the U.S. Trustees crime-victim assistance program to help resolve this case of bankruptcy fraud.

If you have any questions concerning this case or require additional documentation to establish my identity, please don't hesitate to contact me at [work phone] and [home or cell phone] or by e-mail at [e-mail address]. Thank you for your time and attention to this matter.

Sincerely,
Your Name

Sample Letter to Request Medical Records

This sample letter can be used to request medical records if you become suspicious that someone is using your identity to obtain medical care fraudulently (see page 77). You should request a statement from your insurer once a year detailing all benefits paid out for the year. If you see any payouts that are suspicious, contact your insurer and dispute the claim. Also ask your insurer to verify your current address to ensure that an imposter hasn't used your information to change your billing address. You are also entitled under the Health Insurance Portability and Accountability Act to an "accounting of disclosures" from your health insurer or health-care provider (note that you may be charged a small fee to copy the records and for postage if you request to have the documents mailed to your home). The accounting spells out who was given access to your personal records and for what purpose.

You also have the right under federal law to receive a copy of your medical records from your health-care provider, though again you'll likely be charged a small fee. By law, the health-care provider has up to thirty days to respond to your request (the provider can have an additional thirty days if it can document good cause). Many states have enacted their own health privacy laws that govern how much health-care providers can charge and how much time they have to respond to patients' requests for records. The Georgetown University Center on Medical Rights and Privacy has compiled a list of thirty-two state guides to help consumers understand their rights. It can be found at http://hpi.georgetown.edu/privacy/records.html.

After reviewing your records, be sure to keep them in a secure place, as these documents generally include Social Security number, date of birth, insurance records and other extremely sensitive personal information. If you spot any errors or treatments you never received, you may have trouble getting the information removed from your file. However, you can request that the file be amended to include a statement from you that disputes the erroneous information and any evidence you have to support your complaint.

Your Name   Date
Your Address
Your Telephone Number

Health-Insurance Number, Date of Birth or
Medical Record Number

Name of Doctor or Health-Care Provider
Address
Re: Request for Medical Records

Dear Sir or Madam:

I am writing to request copies of my medical records, as is my right under the Health Insurance Portability and Accountability Act. I would like to receive a copy of the entire record, to include all handwritten notes, X-rays and other medical records.

[Note: You may also request a summary of your medical record, which may be advisable if you're a long-time patient of the health-care provider with a lengthy record.]

If there are administrative fees to copy and mail these records to my home address, please contact me at your earliest convenience to discuss the cost. Please inform me in writing if you are unable to fulfill my request within thirty days, as is required under HIPAA.

Sincerely,
Your Name

Sample Letter Reporting a Death to Credit-Reporting Agencies

I know that during a time of bereavement, preventing ID theft isn't the first thing that comes to mind. But using this sample letter to inform credit-reporting agencies about a loved one's death can help prevent the survivors from having to deal with the theft of the deceased's identity. As soon as can be reasonably done, mail copies of this letter and the person's death certificates—certified mail, return-receipt requested—to the three major credit-reporting agencies—Experian, Equifax and

TransUnion—asking that "deceased alerts" be put on the person's files. This should prevent creditors from opening up an account in your loved one's name. (I write "should" because mistakes can be made, and, sadly, some careless creditors overlook such things.) Also request copies of the deceased's files and be sure to contact all creditors listed immediately to inform them of the death.

Your Name   Date
Your Relationship to the Deceased
Your Address
Your Telephone Number

Name of Credit-Reporting Agency
Address

Re: Notice of Death

Dear Sir or Madam:

The purpose of this letter is to inform you of the death of [name, followed by your relationship to the deceased]. Enclosed, please find a copy of [his/her] death certificate.

To identify [name of deceased] and establish my relationship to [him/her], I have provided the following information: [Social Security number, date of birth, any former addresses]. [If you are not the spouse of the deceased, note that fact in the letter and provide a copy of your power of attorney or any documentation establishing you as executor of the estate.]

I am extremely concerned about the threat of identity theft, so I would like to request that a copy of [name of the deceased] credit report be mailed to me. I would also like to have [his/her] file flagged with a "Deceased—Do Not Issue Credit" alert to prevent identity thieves from opening new accounts in [his/her] name.

Thank you for your time and prompt attention to this matter.

Sincerely,
Your Name

IDENTITY THEFT LOGS

U se this log to help track and follow up on correspondence if you've become a victim of identity theft. Keep your log in a binder to store all of your correspondence and copies of every theft-related document you've completed.

Date/Time	Name of Company or Agency Contacted	Full Name of Person Contacted	Contact Numbers or Email
09/01/2006 10:00 AM	ABC credit-card company	Laura Jones, fraud specialist	Phone: (800) 555-1212 Fax: (800) 555-1213 laura.jones@ abccreditcards.com

Action Taken (documents mailed or received, police report filed, etc.)	Time Spent on Task	Total Expense Incurred	Lost Earnings Potential	Follow-up Action Necessary?
Recommended I fill out a fraudulent account statement and send certified mail	30 minutes	$7.50	$10 @ $20 an hour	Company will contact me by Oct. 1 to discuss case

Use this log to help track and follow up on all of your expenses if you've become a victim of identity theft. Keep your log in a

Date/Time	Name of Company or Agency Contacted	Phone Calls	Photo Copies and Other Documentation Costs
09/01/2006 10:00 AM	ABC credit-card company	$2.50	$7.50

binder to store all of your receipts for every theft-related expense you've incurred.

Travel Mileage	Lost Earnings Potential	Notary Signatures	Attorney Fees	Counseling Costs	Other
	$10.00				

The Laws That Protect You

W hat are your protections under federal and state law? Here's a look at significant identity-theft legislation.

FEDERAL

The Identity Theft and Assumption Deterrence Act

This 1998 act made it a federal crime to knowingly transfer or use a means of identification of another person with the intent to commit, or to aid or abet, a federal crime. Violations are investigated by federal agencies, including the U.S. Secret Service, the Federal Bureau of Investigation and the Postal Inspection Service, and are prosecuted by the Department of Justice. An amendment to the act, the Identity Theft Penalty Enhancement Act, established penalties for general identity-theft offenses and for more serious offenses such as impersonating an individual for the purpose of committing an act of terrorism.

The Fair Credit Reporting Act

The Fair Credit Reporting Act enhanced the accuracy and privacy of information kept in consumer credit reports. Later amendments to the act helped to control access to and use of credit reports and required consumer-reporting agencies to maintain correct and complete files. The law gives consumers the right to review credit reports for accuracy and to have incorrect information either verified or corrected in a timely manner. Here are a few of the main consumer protections under the act:

Credit-Reporting Agencies

- Credit-reporting companies are required to make reports easier for consumers to understand and to restrict access to the reports to those with legitimate business interests—generally, lenders, employers, insurers or other parties that you give permission to request a copy of your report.

- Credit bureaus must investigate and change or remove incorrect information. Consumers who don't agree with an investigation's findings have the right to attach brief statements clarifying the disputes.

- Consumers can obtain and review one free credit report annually from each of the three credit-reporting agencies—Experian, Equifax and TransUnion. Requests can be made online at www.annualcreditreport.com or by calling (877) 322-8228. You can also request your free copy by mail at Annual Credit Report Request Service, P.O. Box 105281, Atlanta, GA 30348-5281. (You'll be required to provide a Social Security number for identification.)

- A consumer is also entitled to a free copy of his or her credit report if denied credit based on a credit bureau report. The free report must be requested from the credit bureau that provided the negative consumer information to the creditor within thirty days of the consumer being turned down for credit. Certain unemployed individuals and those on public welfare assistance may also be entitled to free copies of their credit reports.

- After a dispute has been settled, you have the right to have the credit bureau reissue corrected reports free of charge to lenders who received reports within the last six months or to employers who received them in the last two years.

The Fair and Accurate Credit Transactions Act

The law requires merchants to truncate account numbers on all credit-card and debit-card receipts, though it doesn't apply to handwritten receipts or those made with an imprint of a card. Merchants with machines in use prior to January 1, 2005, were given up to three years to comply with the new rules.

The Fair Credit Billing Act

If you've ever been billed for an unauthorized purchase on an open-ended credit line (such as gas or department-store credit cards), your rights are protected under the Fair Credit Billing Act. The act limits consumers' liability for unauthorized charges to $50—though many companies will waive this amount if consumers notify them of the dispute in a timely manner. In addition to fraudulent charges, some of the billing disputes covered are:

- bills that list the wrong date or billing amount;

- charges for goods and services you didn't accept or receive;

- math or computer errors;

- failure to post payments or credits (for example, returned goods);

- bills mailed to the wrong address (provided the creditor receives your change of address, in writing, at least twenty days before the billing period ends); and

- charges for which you ask for an explanation or written proof of purchase along with a claimed error or request for clarification.

The Fair Debt Collection Practices Act

This law was designed to stop unscrupulous debt-collection agencies from making false statements or harassing consumers for outstanding credit-card debt, auto loans, medical bills and other types of unsecured debts. A debt collector is in violation of the law if, among other things, it

- continues to call you after you've requested in writing that it stop;

- threatens violence or uses harsh, profane or abusive language;

- falsely represents who it is or the amount of the debt owed; and

- threatens wage garnishment or seizure of property, unless it has a legal right to do so.

If the law is violated, consumers are allowed to sue collectors in state or federal court for damages suffered plus an additional $1,000 per violation. It doesn't, however, wipe out any legitimate debts you may owe.

The Electronic Fund Transfer Act

While the Fair Credit Billing Act provides protection for revolving credit accounts, the Electronic Fund Transfer Act builds in safeguards for misuse of bank debit cards and reimbursement in the event of lost or stolen cards.

In many instances, you won't be liable for fraudulent purchases made with lost or stolen debit cards. For example, by law, you can't be held responsible if you report a card missing before it's used for unauthorized withdrawals. If you delay, however, you could be in for a nasty surprise:

- If you report the loss within two business days after you realize your card is missing, you can be held liable for up to only $50 for unauthorized purchases. (Regardless of the law, many financial institutions waive this amount—particularly for good customers.)

- If you wait up to sixty days after your statement is mailed to you to report the fraudulent transfer or purchase, you could be responsible for as much as $500.

- If you don't report unauthorized purchases or transfers within sixty days after the statement is mailed to you, you could be on the hook for the entire amount—including your entire bank balance and any line of credit attached to the account for overdraft protection.

Even if you report the loss right away, you could face headaches. In the interim, you may get hit with stop-payment or bounced-check fees while you're waiting for your financial institution to make you whole again.

Another provision allows a consumer to dispute account statement errors within sixty days from the date the monthly statement containing the errors is sent to the account holder. The financial institution then has ten business days to investigate and afterward notify the account holder of its findings within three days. Errors must be corrected within one business day of being detected. If the bank needs more time to investigate, it can take up to an additional forty-five days, but during that time, it must credit your account for the amount in dispute and notify you of the ongoing investigation. If no error is detected after the forty-five days, it must send you written notification that it will debit your account for the disputed amount.

Be warned: If you miss that sixty-day window, you have no additional federal protections. (If you haven't already signed up to view your bank account statements online throughout the month, this is a good reason to start.)

Enhanced Privacy Laws

A number of federal laws protect how personal identifiable information is shared by government entities, financial institutions and the medical community. Among the most notable are the following:

- **The Gramm-Leach-Bliley Act** This act requires financial institutions to notify customers of their privacy policies at least on an annual basis and to allow consumers the opportunity to opt out of unsolicited offers from nonaffiliated third-party companies before disclosing consumers' personal financial information to those companies.

- **The Driver's Privacy Protection Act** This act places limits on state departments of motor vehicles on the disclosure of individual records.

- **The Health Information Portability and Accountability Act** This act protects the security, privacy and confidentiality of patient records and information.

- **Family Educational Rights and Privacy Act** This act limits the use and disclosure of education records by agencies and institutions that receive federal funding.

STATE

States have been far more aggressive than the federal government in creating consumer protections from identity theft. The efforts have been spearheaded by the state of California, which has some of the toughest privacy and identity theft protection laws in the nation.

IDENTITY THEFT STATUTES BY STATE
(As of July 13, 2006)

State	Statutory Citation	Title	Penalty
Alabama	13A-8-190 to 13A-8-201 2006 Act 148	The Consumer Identity Protection Act	Identity theft is a Class C felony Trafficking in stolen identities is a Class B felony Obstructing justice using a false identity is a Class C felony
Alaska	11.46.180	Theft by deception	First degree is a Class B felony Second degree is a Class C felony Third degree is a Class A misdemeanor Fourth degree is a Class B misdemeanor
Arizona	13-2008	Taking identity of another person; classification:	Class 4 felony
	13-2009	Aggravated taking identity of another person or entity; classification:	Class 3 felony
	13-2010	Trafficking in the identity of another person or entity	Class 2 felony
Arkansas	5-37-227	Financial identity fraud	Class C felony
	5-37-228	Identity theft passport	

State	Statutory Citation	Title	Penalty
California	Penal Code 530.5 to 530.8		Upon conviction a person shall be punished either by imprisonment in a county jail not to exceed one year, a fine not to exceed $1,000, or both that imprisonment and fine, or by imprisonment in the state prison, a fine not to exceed $10,000, or both that imprisonment and fine.
			Every person who, with the intent to defraud, acquires, transfers, or retains possession of the personal identifying information of another person is guilty of a public offense, and upon conviction therefor, shall be punished by imprisonment in a county jail not to exceed one year, or a fine not to exceed $1,000, or by both that imprisonment and fine.
			Every person who, with the intent to defraud, acquires, transfers, or retains possession of the personal identifying information, as defined in subdivision (b), of another person who is deployed to a location outside of the state is guilty of a public offense, and upon conviction therefor, shall be punished by imprisonment in a county jail not to exceed one year, or a fine not to exceed $1,500, or by both that imprisonment and fine.

State	Statutory Citation	Title	Penalty
Colorado	18-5-901 *et seq.* 2006 Chap. 289	Identity theft Criminal possession of a financial device Gathering identity information by deception Possession of identity theft tools	Class 4 felony Criminal possession of one financial device is a Class 1 misdemeanor Criminal possession of two or more financial devices is a Class 6 felony Criminal possession of four or more financial devices, of which at least two are issued to different account holders, is a Class 5 felony Class 5 felony Class 5 felony
Connecticut	53a-129a *et seq.*	Identity theft in the first degree Identity theft in the second degree Identity theft in the third degree Trafficking in personal identifying information	Class B felony—the value of the money, credit, goods, services or property obtained exceeds $10,000 Class C felony—the value of the money, credit, goods, services or property obtained exceeds $5,000 Class D felony Class D felony
Delaware	11 §828 11 §854 11 §854a 2006 Chap. 338	Possession of burglar's tools or instruments facilitating theft Identity theft Identity theft passport; application; issuance	Class F felony Class D felony Class D felony
District of Columbia	22-3227.01 to 3227.08	Identity theft in the first degree	Any person convicted of identity theft shall be fined not more than (1) $10,000, (2) three times the value of the property obtained, or (3) three times the amount

State	Statutory Citation	Title	Penalty
District of Columbia (continued)			of the financial injury, whichever is greatest, or imprisoned for not more than 10 years, or both, if the property obtained or the amount of the financial injury is $250 or more.
		Identity theft in the second degree	Any person convicted of identity theft shall be fined not more than $1,000 or imprisoned for not more than 180 days, or both, if the value of the property obtained or the amount of the financial injury, whichever is greater, is less than $250.
		Enhanced penalty	Any person who commits the offense of identity theft against an individual who is 65 years of age or older, at the time of the offense, may be punished by a fine of up to 1½ times the maximum fine otherwise authorized for the offense and may be imprisoned for a term of up to 1½ times the maximum term of imprisonment otherwise authorized for the offense, or both.
Florida	817.568	Criminal use of personal identification information	817.568(2)(a) Third degree felony 817.568(2)(b) Second degree felony 817.568(2)(c) First degree felony 817.568(4) First degree misdemeanor 817.568(5) reclassification 817.568(6) Second degree felony

State	Statutory Citation	Title	Penalty
Florida (continued)			817.568(7) Second degree felony 817.568(8)(a) Third degree felony 817.568(8)(b) Second degree felony 817.568(8)(c) First degree felony 817.568(9) Third degree felony 817.568(10) reclassification
Georgia	16-9-121 to 16-9-128	Financial identity fraud	Punishable by imprisonment for not less than one nor more than 10 years or a fine not to exceed $100,000, or both for first offense Punishable by imprisonment for not less than three nor more than 15 years, a fine not to exceed $250,000, or both for subsequent offenses
Hawaii	708.839.6	Identity theft in the first degree	Class A felony
	708.839.7	Identity theft in the second degree	Class B felony
	708-839.8	Identity theft in the third degree	Class C felony
	2006 Act 139	Unauthorized possession of confidential personal information	Class C felony
Idaho	18-3124	Fraudulent use of a financial transaction card or number	Any person found guilty of a violation of section 18-3124, 18-3125A, 18-3126 or 18-3127, Idaho Code, is guilty of a misdemeanor. In the event that the retail value of the goods obtained or attempted to be obtained through any violation of the provisions
	18-3125	Criminal possession of financial transaction card, financial transaction number and FTC forgery devices	

State	Statutory Citation	Title	Penalty
Idaho (continued)	18-3125A	Unauthorized factoring of credit card sales drafts	of section 18-3124, 18-3125A, 18-3126 or 18-3127, Idaho Code, exceeds $300, any such violation will constitute a felony, and will be punished as provided in this section. Any person found guilty of a violation of section 18-3126A, Idaho Code, is guilty of a felony. For purposes of this section, the punishment for a misdemeanor shall be a fine of up to $1,000 or up to one year in the county jail, or both such fine and imprisonment. For purposes of this section, the punishment for a felony shall be a fine of up to $50,000 or imprisonment in the state prison not exceeding five years, or both such fine and imprisonment.
	18-3126	Misappropriation of personal identifying information	
	18-3126A	Acquisition of personal identifying information by false authority	
	18-3127	Receiving or possessing fraudulently obtained goods or services	
	18-3128	Penalty for violation	
Illinois	720 ILCS 5/16G-1 to 720 ILCS 5/16G-25	Identity theft	Class 4 felony if under $300 in value for first offense Class 3 felony for subsequent offense Class 3 felony if between $300 and $2,000 Class 2 felony if between $2,000 and $10,000 Class 1 felony if between $10,000 and $100,000
	2006 P.A. 94-0827	Methamphetamine enhancement	Class X felony if exceeds $100,000 Class 2 felony for first offense and Class 1 felony for subsequent felonies
	2006 P.A. 94-0969	Aggravated identity theft	Class 3 felony if under $300 in value

State	Statutory Citation	Title	Penalty
Illinois (continued)		Transmission of personal identifying information Facilitating identity theft	Class 2 felony if between $300 and $10,000 Class 1 felony if between $10,000 and $100,000 Class X felony if exceeds $100,000 Class A misdemeanor Class A misdemeanor for first offense and Class 4 felony for subsequent offenses
Indiana	35-43-5-1 34-43-5-3.5 2006 P.L. 125	Definitions Identity Deception	Class D felony The offense defined in subsection (a) is a Class C felony if (1) a person obtains, possesses, transfers, or uses the identifying information of more than 100 persons; or (2) the fair market value of the fraud or harm caused by the offense is at least $50,000
Iowa	614.4A 714.16B 715A-8 et seq. 715A.9A 2006 H.F. 2506	Identity theft Identity theft passport	Aggravated misdemeanor if under $1,000 Class D felony if exceeds $1,000
Kansas	21-3830 21-4018 2006 S.B. 196	Vital records identity fraud Identity theft	Severity level 8, nonperson felony Severity level 8, nonperson felony Severity level 5, nonperson felony if monetary loss is more than $100,000
Kentucky	514.160 514.170	Theft of identity Trafficking in stolen identities	Class D felony Class C felony If a business commits either crime, the business also violates the Consumer Protection Act

State	Statutory Citation	Title	Penalty
Louisiana	RS 14:67.16 2006 Act 241	Identity theft	Punishable by imprisonment for not more than six months or fined not more than $500 if the value of the loss is less than $300. Punishable by imprisonment for not more than three years, with or without hard labor, or fined not more than $3,000 for subsequent offenses. Punishable by imprisonment, with or without hard labor, for not more than one year, or fined not more than $500, or both when the victim is at least 60 or disabled. Punishable by imprisonment for not less than six months and not more than three years, with or without hard labor, or fined not more than $3,000 for subsequent offenses. Punishable by imprisonment, with or without hard labor, for not more than three years, or fined not more than $3,000, or both if between $300 and $500. Punishable by imprisonment, with or without hard labor, for not less than six months and for not more than three years, or fined not more than $3,000, or both when the victim is at least 60 or disabled. Punishable by imprisonment, with or without hard labor, for not more than five years, or fined

State	Statutory Citation	Title	Penalty
Louisiana *(continued)*			not more than $5,000, or both if between $500 and $1,000. Punishable by imprisonment, with or without hard labor, for not less than one year and for not more than five years, or fined not more than $5,000, or both when the victim is at least 60 or disabled. Punishable by imprisonment, with or without hard labor, for not more than 10 years, or fined not more than $10,000, or both if $1,000 or more. Punishable by imprisonment, with or without hard labor, for not less than two years and for not more than 10 years, or fined not more than $10,000, or both when the victim is at least 60 or disabled.
Maine	17-A §905-A	Misuse of identification	Class D crime
Maryland	Criminal Law §8-301 to §8-305	Identity fraud	Misdemeanor where the benefit, credit, good, service, or other thing of value has a value of less than $500; punishable by imprisonment not to exceed 18 months or a fine not exceeding $5,000, or both
		Intent to manufacture, distribute or dispense identities	Felony where the benefit, credit, good, service, or other thing of value has a value of $500 or greater; punishable by imprisonment not to exceed five years or a fine not

State	Statutory Citation	Title	Penalty
Maryland *(continued)*	2006 Chap. 607	Identity theft passport	exceeding $25,000, or both Felony; punishable by imprisonment not to exceed five years or a fine not exceeding $25,000, or both
Massachusetts	266 §37E	Use of personal identification of another; identity fraud; penalty; restitution	Whoever, with intent to defraud, poses as another person without the express authorization of that person and uses such person's personal identifying information to obtain or to attempt to obtain money, credit, goods, services, anything of value, any identification card or other evidence of such person's identity, or to harass another shall be guilty of identity fraud and shall be punished by a fine of not more than $5,000 or imprisonment in a house of correction for not more than two and one-half years, or by both such fine and imprisonment. Whoever, with intent to defraud, obtains personal identifying information about another person without the express authorization of such person, with the intent to pose as such person or who obtains personal identifying information about a person without the express authorization of such person in order to assist another to pose as such

State	Statutory Citation	Title	Penalty
Massachusetts (continued)			person in order to obtain money, credit, goods, services, anything of value, any identification card or other evidence of such person's identity, or to harass another shall be guilty of the crime of identity fraud and shall be punished by a fine of not more than $5,000 or imprisonment in a house of correction for not more than two and one-half years, or by both such fine and imprisonment.
Michigan	445.61 et seq.	Identity Theft Protection Act	Subject to subsection 6, a person who violates section 5 or 7 is guilty of a felony punishable by imprisonment for not more than five years or a fine of not more than $25,000, or both.
Minnesota	609.527	Identity theft	If the offense involves a single direct victim and the total, combined loss to the direct victim and any indirect victims is $250 or less, the person may be sentenced to imprisonment not more than 90 days or fined not more than $700, or both. If the offense involves a single direct victim and the total, combined loss to the direct victim and any indirect victims is more than $250 but not more than $500, the person may be sentenced to imprisonment for not more than one year or to payment of a

State	Statutory Citation	Title	Penalty
Minnesota *(continued)*			fine of not more than $3,000, or both. If the offense involves two or three direct victims or the total, combined loss to the direct and indirect victims is more than $500 but not more than $2,500, the person may be sentenced to imprisonment for not more than five years or to payment of a fine of not more than $10,000, or both. If the offense involves four or more direct victims, or if the total, combined loss to the direct and indirect victims is more than $2,500, the person may be sentenced to imprisonment for not more than ten years or to payment of a fine or not more than $20,000, or both.
Mississippi	97-19-85	Fraudulent use of identity, Social Security number, credit card or debit card number or other identifying information to obtain thing of value	Guilty of a felony and upon conviction thereof for a first offense shall be fined not more than $5,000 or imprisoned for a term not to exceed five years, or both. For a second or subsequent offense such person, upon conviction, shall be fined not more than $10,000 or imprisoned for a term not to exceed 10 years, or both.
	97-45-1 *et seq.*	Computer crimes and identity theft	Guilty of a felony punishable by imprisonment for not less than two nor more than 15 years or a fine of not more than $10,000, or both. If the
	97-45-29	Identity theft passport	

State	Statutory Citation	Title	Penalty
Mississippi (continued)			violation involves an amount of less than $250, a person who violates this section may be found guilty of a misdemeanor punishable by imprisonment in the county jail for a term of not more than six months, or by a fine of not more than $1,000, or both, in the discretion of the court
Missouri	570.223	Identity theft—penalty—restitution Trafficking in stolen identities, crime of—possession of documents, exemptions—violations, penalty	(1) Identity theft or attempted identity theft which does not result in the theft or appropriation of credit, money, goods, services, or other property is a class B misdemeanor; (2) Identity theft which results in the theft or appropriation of credit, money, goods, services, or other property not exceeding $500 in value is a class A misdemeanor; (3) Identity theft which results in the theft or appropriation of credit, money, goods, services, or other property exceeding $500 and not exceeding $5,000 in value is a class C felony; (4) Identity theft which results in the theft or appropriation of credit, money, goods, services, or other property exceeding $5,000 and not exceeding $50,000 in value is a class B felony; (5) Identity theft which results in the theft or

State	Statutory Citation	Title	Penalty
Missouri (continued)			appropriation of credit, money, goods, services, or other property exceeding $50,000 in value is a class A felony.
Montana	45-6-332 46-24-220	Theft of identity Identity theft passport	If no economic benefit was gained or was attempted to be gained or if an economic benefit of less than $1,000 was gained or attempted to be gained, punishable by fine in an amount not to exceed $1,000, imprisonment in the county jail for a term not to exceed six months, or both. If an economic benefit of $1,000 or more was gained or attempted to be gained, punishable by fine an amount not to exceed $10,000, imprisonment in a state prison for a term not to exceed 10 years, or both.
Nebraska	28-608	Criminal impersonation; penalty; restitution	Class II misdemeanor if no credit, money, goods, services, or other thing of value was gained or was attempted to be gained, or if the credit, money, goods, services, or other thing of value that was gained or was attempted to be gained was less than $200. Any second conviction under this subdivision is a Class I misdemeanor, and any third or subsequent conviction under this subdivision is a Class IV felony. Class I misdemeanor if

State	Statutory Citation	Title	Penalty
Nebraska (continued)			the credit, money, goods, services, or other thing of value that was gained or was attempted to be gained was $200 or more but less than $500. Any second or subsequent conviction under this subdivision is a Class IV felony. Class IV felony if the credit, money, goods, services, or other thing of value that was gained or was attempted to be gained was $500 or more but less than $1,500. Class III felony if the credit, money, goods, services, or other thing of value that was gained or was attempted to be gained was $1,500 or more.
Nevada	205.461 *et seq.*	Obtaining and using personal identifying information of another person to harm person or for unlawful purpose	Category B felony or Category E felony
	205.464	Obtaining, using, possessing or selling personal identifying information for unlawful purpose by public officer or public employee	Category B felony if victim is an older person or vulnerable adult
	205.465	Possession or sale of document or personal identifying information	Category B felony or Category C felony

State	Statutory Citation	Title	Penalty
Nevada *(continued)*		to establish false status or identity	
	205.4651	Identity theft passport	Category C felony or Category E felony Category B felony if victim is an older person or vulnerable adult
New Hampshire	638:25 to 638:27	Identity fraud	Class A felony
New Jersey	2C:21-17 to 2C:21-17.6	Impersonation; theft of identity; crime	If the actor obtains a benefit or deprives another of a benefit in an amount less than $500 and the offense involves the identity of one victim, the actor shall be guilty of a crime of the fourth degree except that a second or subsequent conviction for such an offense constitutes a crime of the third degree.
		Use of personal identifying information of another, certain; second degree crime	If the actor obtains a benefit or deprives another of a benefit in an amount of at least $500 but less than $75,000, or the offense involves the identity of at least two but less than five victims, the actor shall be guilty of a crime of the third degree;
		Trafficking in personal identifying information pertaining to another person, certain; crime degrees; terms defined	If the actor obtains a benefit or deprives another of a benefit in the amount of $75,000 or more, or the offense involves the identity of five or more victims, the actor shall be guilty of a crime of the second degree Crime of the fourth degree—one item pertaining to another person

State	Statutory Citation	Title	Penalty
New Jersey *(continued)*			Crime of the third degree—20 items pertaining to five or more separate persons Crime of the second degree—50 items pertaining to five or more separate persons
New Mexico	30-16-24.1	Theft of identity Obtaining identity by electronic fraud	Fourth degree felony Fourth degree felony
New York	Penal Code 190.77 to 190.84	Identity theft in the third degree Identity theft in the second degree Identity theft in the first degree Unlawful possession of personal identifying information in the third degree Unlawful possession of personal identifying information in the second degree Unlawful possession of personal identifying information in the first degree	190.78 Class A misdemeanor 190.79 Class E felony 190.80 Class D felony 190.81 Class A misdemeanor 190.82 Class E felony 190.83 Class D felony
North Carolina	14-113.20 to 14-113.23	Identity Theft	Punishable as a Class G felony, except it is punishable as a Class F felony if: (i) the victim suffers arrest, detention, or conviction as a proximate result of the offense, or (ii) the person is in possession of the identifying information pertaining to three or more separate persons

State	Statutory Citation	Title	Penalty
North Carolina (continued)		Trafficking in stolen identities	Punishable as a Class E felony
North Dakota	12.1-23-11	Unauthorized use of personal identifying information—Penalty	Class B felony if the credit, money, goods, services, anything else of value exceeds $1,000 in value, otherwise the offense is a Class C felony. A second or subsequent offense is a Class A felony.
Ohio	2913.49 109.94	Identity fraud Identity fraud against an elderly person or disabled adult	Fifth degree felony unless: 1) If the value of the credit, property, services, debt, or other legal obligation involved in the violation or course of conduct is $500 or more and is less than $5,000, identity fraud is a felony of the fourth degree. 2) If the value of the credit, property, services, debt, or other legal obligation involved in the violation or course of conduct is $5,000 or more and is less than $100,000, identity fraud is a felony of the third degree. 3) If the value of the credit, property, services, debt, or other legal obligation involved in the violation or course of conduct is $100,000 or more, identity fraud is a felony of the second degree.
		Identity theft passport	Fifth degree felony unless: 1) If the value of the credit, property, services, debt, or other legal obligation involved in the violation or course of conduct is

State	Statutory Citation	Title	Penalty
Ohio (continued)			$500 or more and is less than $5,000, identity fraud is a felony of the third degree. 2) If the value of the credit, property, services, debt, or other legal obligation involved in the violation or course of conduct is $5,000 or more and is less than $100,000, identity fraud is a felony of the second degree. 3) If the value of the credit, property, services, debt, or other legal obligation involved in the violation or course of conduct is $100,000 or more, identity fraud is a felony of the first degree.
Oklahoma	21 §1533.1 22-19b	Identity theft Identity theft passport	Felony offense punishable by imprisonment for a period not to exceed two years, or a fine not to exceed $100,000, or by both such fine and imprisonment.
Oregon	165.800	Identity theft	Class C felony
Pennsylvania	18 Pa.C.S.A. §4120	Identity theft	If the total value involved is less than $2,000, the offense is a misdemeanor of the first degree. If the total value involved is $2,000 or more, the offense is a felony of the third degree. Regardless of the total value involved, if the offense is committed in furtherance of a criminal conspiracy, as defined in section 903, the offense is a felony of the third degree. Regardless of the total

State	Statutory Citation	Title	Penalty
Pennsylvania (continued)			value involved, if the offense is a third or subsequent offense, the offense is a felony of the second degree.
Rhode Island	11-49.1-1 to 11-49.1-5	Impersonation and Identity Fraud Act	First offense punishable by imprisonment for not more than three years and may be fined not more than $5,000, or both. Second offense punishable by imprisonment for not less than three years nor more than five years and shall be fined not more than $10,000, or both. Subsequent offense punishable by imprisonment for not less than five years nor more than 10 years and shall be fined not less than $15,000, or both.
South Carolina	16-13-500 to 16-13-530	Personal Financial Security Act	Felony; must be fined in the discretion of the court or imprisoned not more than 10 years, or both.
South Dakota	22-40-1 et seq.	Identity theft	Class 6 felony
Tennessee	39-14-150	Identity theft Identity theft trafficking	Class D felony Class C felony
	39-16-303	Using a false identification	Class C misdemeanor
Texas	Penal Code 32.51	Fraudulent Use or Possession of Identifying Information	State jail felony
	Business & Commerce Code 48.001 et seq.	Identity Theft Enforcement and Protection Act	

State	Statutory Citation	Title	Penalty
Utah	76-6-1101 to 76-6-1104	Identity fraud	Third degree felony if the value of the credit, goods, services, or any other thing of value is less than $5,000 Second degree felony if the value of the credit, goods, services, or any other thing of value is or exceeds $5,000
		Unlawful possession of another's identification documents	Class A misdemeanor or third degree felony
Vermont	13 §2030	Identity theft	A person who violates this section shall be imprisoned for not more than three years or fined not more $5,000, or both. A person who is convicted of a second or subsequent violation of this section involving a separate scheme shall be imprisoned for not more than ten years or fined not more than $10,000, or both.
Virginia	18.2-152.5:1	Using a computer to gather identifying information; penalties	Any person who violates this section is guilty of a Class 6 felony. Any person who violates this section and sells or distributes such information to another is guilty of a Class 5 felony. Any person who violates this section and uses such information in the commission of another crime is guilty of a Class 5 felony.
	18.2-186.3	Identity theft; penalty; restitution; victim assistance	Class 1 misdemeanor Any violation resulting in financial loss of greater than $200 shall be punishable as a Class 6

State	Statutory Citation	Title	Penalty
Virginia *(continued)*			felony. Any second or-subsequent conviction shall be punishable as a Class 6 felony.
	18.2-186.3:1	Identity fraud; consumer reporting agencies; police reports	Any violation of subsection B where five or more persons' identifying information has been obtained, recorded, or accessed in the same transaction or occurrence shall be punishable as a Class 6 felony. Any violation of subsection B where 50 or more persons' identifying information has been obtained, recorded, or accessed in the same transaction or occurrence shall be punishable as a Class 5 felony.
	18.2-186.5	Expungement of false identity information from police and court records; Identity Theft Passport	Any violation resulting in the arrest and detention of the person whose identification documents or identifying information were used to avoid summons, arrest, prosecution, or to impede a criminal investigation shall be punishable as a Class 6 felony.
Washington	9.35.001 to 9.35-902	Improperly obtaining financial information Identity theft	Class C felony Violation of this section when the accused or an accomplice uses the victim's means of identification or financial information and obtains an aggregate total of credit, money, goods, services, or anything else of value in excess of $1,500 in value shall constitute identity theft in the first

State	Statutory Citation	Title	Penalty
Washington (continued)			degree. Identity theft in the first degree is a class B felony. Violation of this section when the accused or an accomplice uses the victim's means of identification or financial information and obtains an aggregate total of credit, money, goods, services, or anything else of value that is less than $1,500 in value, or when no credit, money, goods, services, or anything of value is obtained shall constitute identity theft in the second degree. Identity theft in the second degree is a class C felony.
West Virginia	61-3-54	Taking identity of another person; penalty	Felony; punished by confinement in the penitentiary not more than five years, or fined not more than $1,000, or both
Wisconsin	943.201	Misappropriation of personal identifying information or personal identification documents	Class H felony
Wyoming	6-3-901	Unauthorized use of personal identifying information; penalties; restitution	A misdemeanor punishable by imprisonment for not more than six months, a fine of not more than $750, or both, if no economic benefit was gained or was attempted to be gained, or if an economic benefit of less than $1,000 was gained or was attempted to be gained

State	Statutory Citation	Title	Penalty
Wyoming *(continued)*			A felony punishable by imprisonment for not more than 10 years, a fine of not more than $10,000, or both, if an economic benefit of $500.00 or more was gained or was attempted to be gained

Source: National Conference of State Legislatures
http://www.ncsl.org/programs/lis/privacy/idt-statutes.htm

This list is just a sampling of some of the protections, but new laws and amendments to old laws are being crafted every day. To keep up on the latest federal, state and local laws and amendments regarding identity theft, check out the Federal Trade Commission's consumer Web site at www.consumer. gov/idtheft/law_laws.htm or that of consumer-advocacy group Privacy Rights Clearinghouse at www.privacyrights.org.

INDEX

ABOUT THE AUTHOR

TERRI CULLEN is an award-winning Personal Finance Columnist for *The Wall Street Journal Online.* She's Assistant Managing Editor of the online Journal and was one of the original journalists hired to launch the premier financial-news Web site back in 1995. Terri is also a contributor to *The Wall Street Journal Online's Guide to Online Investing: How to Make the Most of the Internet in a Bull or Bear Market.* She lives on the Jersey Shore with her husband, Gerry, and son, Gerald, and on sunny summer weekends you'll find them on their boat chasing stripers off the coast.

GET YOUR FINANCIAL LIFE IN ORDER WITH THE MOST TRUSTED NAME IN THE WORLD OF FINANCE.

The Wall Street Journal Guide to the Business of Life is both an instruction manual for living life to the fullest and a fun read about what really matters in the day-to-day.

The Wall Street Journal. Guide to the Business of Life
1-4000-8159-9, $27.50 (Canada: $39.95)

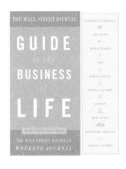

Up-to-date and expertly written, *The Wall Street Journal. Complete Money & Investing Guidebook* provides investors with a simple—but not simplistic—grounding in the world of finance.

The Wall Street Journal. Complete Money & Investing Guidebook
0-307-23699-4, $14.95 paper (Canada: $21.00)

The quintessential primer on understanding and managing your money, this indispensable book takes the mystery out of personal finance.

The Wall Street Journal. Complete Personal Finance Guidebook
0-307-33600-X, $14.95 paper (Canada: $21.00)

This hands-on, interactive guide to managing your personal finances makes it quick and easy to get your financial life in order and ultimately build wealth.

The Wall Street Journal. Personal Finance Workbook
0-307-33601-8, $13.95 paper (Canada: $21.00)